The
BATTLES
OF
ST ALBANS

Michael Elliot

Harvey B. Watson

Battleground: Wars of the Roses

The BATTLES OF ST ALBANS

PETER BURLEY, MICHAEL ELLIOTT
and HARVEY WATSON

Pen & Sword
MILITARY

First published in Great Britain in 2007 by
Pen & Sword Military
an imprint of
Pen & Sword Books Ltd
47 Church Street
Barnsley
South Yorkshire
S70 2AS

ISBN 978-1-844-15569-9

A CIP catalogue record for this book is
available from the British Library.

Graham Turner's painting of the First Battle of St Albans, a detail from which is
reproduced on the cover (the complete image can be seen in the colour plate
section), is available as a fine art print, forming part of a range of prints and
cards published from Graham Turner's historical art. A free colour catalogue is
available from Studio 88 Ltd., P.O. Box 568, Aylesbury, Bucks, HP17 8ZX, phone
and fax 01296 338504 – or log on to www.studio88.co.uk for details of the full
range and Graham's original paintings.

Typeset in ITC Century by Phoenix Typesetting, Auldgirth, Dumfriesshire

Printed and bound in Great Britain by CPI UK

Pen & Sword Books Ltd incorporates the imprints of Pen & Sword Aviation, Pen
& Sword Maritime, Pen & Sword Military, Wharncliffe Local History, Pen and
Sword Select, Pen and Sword Military Classics and Leo Cooper.

For a complete list of Pen & Sword titles, please contact
Pen & Sword Books Limited
47 Church Street, Barnsley, South Yorkshire, S70 2AS, England
E-mail: enquiries@pen-and-sword.co.uk
Website: www.pen-and-sword.co.uk

Contents

ACKNOWLEDGEMENTS

A work of this nature cannot be achieved without the help and support of many others. The authors therefore express their grateful thanks to (among others): Rupert Harding of Pen & Sword for his sustained enthusiasm and encouragement for this project; John Kliene and Peter Shepherd for their photographic skills; Martyn Smith and other members of John Nesfield's Retinue for their willingness to be the subjects of many photographs and their welcome at several events and also members of other re-enactment groups associated with Livery & Maintenance; John Beckerson, Kate Warren, Claire Thornton, Elanor Cowland and Brian Adams of St Albans Museums for their invaluable assistance in tracking down and making available images from the museums' collections; Margaret Wilson from St Peter's Church, St Albans; Janet Sidaway and Tim Barnes for rendering some very difficult Latin into plain English; the Meteorological Office for their insight into the weather conditions in February 1461; members of the St Albans and Hertfordshire Architectural and Archaeological Society for support and for guidance on local sources; the Hertfordshire Library Service for tracking down and providing some of the more important local texts; and the other members of the London Branch of the Battlefields Trust for their encouragement and support.

This book would have been much poorer (and less accurate) without the myriad insights into fifteenth-century St Albans by Rosalind Niblett and Isobel Thompson in their major study of local archaeology, fortuitously published in late 2005.

Last and certainly not least, thanks are due to Alison and Jenny for putting up with their husbands (Mike and Peter respectively) endlessly going on about the battles for the last year and a half!

Without your help this book would not have been possible – our sincere thanks to you all.

OUTLINE CHRONOLOGY LOCATING THE BATTLES IN THE WARS OF THE ROSES

1399	Henry Bolingbroke seizes throne and is crowned Henry IV. Dynastic origin of the wars.
1413	Henry V accedes to the throne. Lancastrian dynasty confirmed.
1422	Henry VI accedes to the throne (reigns 1422–61 and 1470–1). Long minority followed by weak rule, no heirs (to 1453) and loss of France.
1452	York's first bid for power at Blackheath (failed). Scene set for struggle of Houses of York and Beaufort.
1453	Battle of Castillon. End of Hundred Years War, loss of all English possessions in France except Calais, and Lancastrians discredited.
1453	Henry VI's mental collapse and York appointed Protector. Apparent triumph of York.
1453	Birth of Edward of Lancaster. Lancastrian dynasty gains a future.
1454	Henry VI recovers, Somerset appointed Protector instead. Coup d'état seems to end Yorkist hopes, York himself in danger.
1455 (22 May)	First Battle of St Albans, York reappointed Protector. Yorkists take military action to eliminate Lancastrian power.
1456	Henry VI recovers, York loses Protectorship. Political benefits from First Battle of St Albans lost.
1456–59	Lancastrians take over all the the reins of power. Yorkists facing political elimination, York goes into exile in Ireland.
1459	Second phase of the wars begins. Yorkist victory at Battle of Blore Heath.

1459 (October)	(Battle of) Ludford Bridge. Complete collapse of Yorkist military position and withdrawal from England.
1460 (July)	Yorkists invade England, Battle of Northampton, capture of London and of Henry VI. Yorkists regain the ascendancy, but York's attempt to seize the throne fails.
1460 (December)	Battle of Wakefield, York killed in worst Yorkist defeat to date. Lancastrians poised to regain the ascendancy and invade the south.
1461 (Jan.–Feb.)	Lancastrian army marches south. Devastation caused was a major political blunder.
1461 (2–3 Feb.)	Battle of Mortimer's Cross. Yorkists secure Wales and the west in apparent side-show.
1461 (17 Feb.)	Second Battle of St Albans, Henry VI recaptured. Apparent elimination of main Yorkist army, end of wars in sight.
1461 (late Feb.)	Lancastrians fail to capture London, Earl of March relieves London, Lancastrians retreat north. Fruits of victory at St Albans lost and next campaign ensues.
1461 (1 March)	Earl of March proclaimed king. Formal start of Yorkist dynasty.
1461 (27–29 March)	Battles of Ferrybridge and Towton. Elimination of Lancastrian army, capture of Henry VI, confirmation of Edward IV as king. End of this phase of the wars.
1469	Third phase of the wars begins. Warwick rebels against Edward IV.
1470–1	Warwick briefly restores Henry VI.
1471	Battles of Barnet and Tewkesbury. Warwick defeated and killed by Edward IV (Barnet), Edward of Lancaster killed (Tewkesbury), and Henry VI murdered.
1483	Death of Edward IV and accession of Edward V and then Richard III. Thirteen-year-old Edward V deposed by his uncle Richard of Gloucester. Edward and younger brother disappear (probably murdered by Richard III). Opposition to Richard III initiates fourth phase of the wars.

| 1485 | Battle of Bosworth, end of Yorkist dynasty, accession of Henry VII. Richard III defeated and killed by Henry Tudor, who becomes Henry VII and marries Edward IV's daughter (Elizabeth of York), uniting the two Houses. |
| 1487 | Battle of Stoke. Rebellion against Henry VII defeated in the last major battle of the wars. |

Diary for 22 May 1455

This is a conjectural outline schedule of the sequence of events on the day, given that the timings in the different chronicles are not complete or consistent.

Midnight to dawn	Armies both marching on St Albans and exchanging messages.
3 a.m. – 7 a.m.	Lancastrians and then Yorkists reach St Albans.
7 a.m. – 10 a.m.	Further negotiations, Yorkists prepare for combat (but most Lancastrians do not).
10 a.m.	First Yorkist attack (on Sopwell and Shropshire Lane Bars).
10–10.30 a.m.	Yorkist attacks held, stalemate in prospect.
10.30 a.m.	Warwick and Ogle lead attack through the town backsides into the Market Place.
10.30–11 a.m.	Fierce fighting in the Market Place and Town Square with Henry VI wounded and captured and Somerset, Northumberland and Clifford killed.
11 a.m.	End of fighting with Lancastrian army and its commanders eliminated. Lancastrians not dead or wounded disperse.
Afternoon	Town pillaged; Henry VI taken to Abbey; York reappointed as Protector; Lancastrian wounded taken into custody and the dead disposed of.

Diary for 17 February 1461

This is a conjectural outline schedule – based only on known events – of the sequence of events on the day, given that the timings in the different chronicles are not complete or consistent.

Midnight to dawn	Lancastrians marching down Watling Street from Dunstable, Yorkists staying in fortified positions and in town.
Dawn	First Lancastrian attack from St Michael's up Fishpool Street to Market Place.
Early to mid-morning	Lancastrian attack held and rest of army reaches St Michael's.
Late morning	Second Lancastrian attack up Catherine Lane to St Peter's.
Noon	Yorkists in town surrounded and eliminated, Lancastrian attack turns north towards main Yorkist forces on Bernards Heath.
Early afternoon	Fierce fighting on Bernards Heath as Montagu tries to hold off the Lancastrian attack.
Mid-afternoon	Montagu's forces overwhelmed; he, Lord Berners and Henry VI captured; Kentish contingent defects; Yorkist front line disintegrates.
Late afternoon	Warwick leads an unsuccessful counter-attack, Yorkists disperse and retreat.
Evening	Warwick draws off to the north in a fighting retreat with the rump of his army, Lancastrians too exhausted to pursue. Henry VI taken to Abbey and Lancastrian power seems restored.

Introduction

The city of St Albans is one of the oldest towns in England, with an eventful and colourful history stretching back over 2,000 years to the Iron Age. In that time it has witnessed many scenes of great drama and tragedy, such as the first century AD when Boudicca and her followers sacked the Roman settlement of Verulamium, or the third century AD when a Roman citizen named Alban was prepared to die for his beliefs, thus becoming Britain's first Christian martyr. In the fifteenth century St Albans again became the centre of violent conflict when the medieval town was the site of two bloody battles. The first was fought on 22 May 1455, and marked the beginning of that confused and turbulent period in English history known as the Wars of the Roses. Following the battle the town was sacked and pillaged. Scarcely had St Albans recovered from this catastrophe, when, less than six years later, the Second Battle of St Albans was fought, on Shrove Tuesday, 17 February 1461. The second battle proved to be an even greater bloodbath than the first, with far more men involved and a far greater number of casualties. This book tells the story of these two epic battles, when for a brief moment of history St Albans found itself at the very centre of the struggle between the Houses of York and Lancaster.

Few events in English history have been so distorted by myth and legend as the Wars of the Roses. For over thirty years England was torn apart by a violent struggle between rival claimants to the throne. From the sons of King Edward III had sprung several great families, among them the Houses of York and Lancaster. Each House believed that it had a legitimate claim to the throne. Each House needed the support of the powerful barons and nobles of the nation, who were greedy for wealth and power. These noblemen were often willing to support either side, or even to change sides if they thought it might benefit them. Contrary to popular belief, the wars had nothing to do with the traditional feuds between the counties of Yorkshire and Lancashire. If there was a geographical element to the wars, it was because most of the Lancastrian support came from the north of England and much of the Yorkist support was in the south.

Even the name 'The Wars of the Roses' is misleading, and was not commonly used by historians until the nineteenth century. It derives from the fact that the Yorkists are supposed to have used the white rose as a badge and the Lancastrians the red rose. However, various badges, symbols and coats of arms were used

1

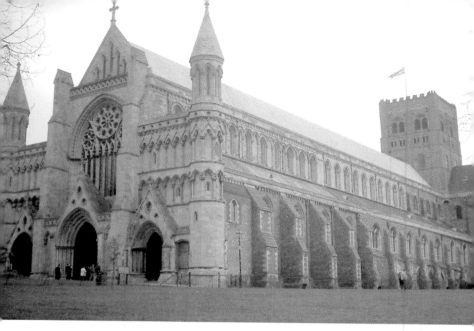

The Abbey – iconic symbol of St Albans now as it was then. *Mike Elliott*

during the wars, and the significance of the white and red roses was much exaggerated by later Tudor historians. Many of our ideas about the Wars of the Roses are derived from Shakespeare's plays, but it is important to remember that the plays have more to do with staging good drama and reflecting Tudor propaganda than giving an accurate portrayal of history.

Although the wars lasted some thirty-two years, from the First Battle of St Albans in 1455, to the Battle of Stoke Field in 1487, much of England remained relatively peaceful and prosperous. Most of the fighting occurred during five distinct phases in 1455, 1459 to 1464, 1469 to 1471, 1485 and 1487. Outside of these phases there were long periods of uneasy peace. The ranks of the nobility were decimated during the wars, but the rest of the country remained reasonably prosperous.

It is tempting to dismiss the wars as a crude, brutal power struggle, entirely devoid of political principle or idealism. In fact there was much more to the conflict than this simple analysis would suggest. The fifteenth century was a time of enormous change; a series of intellectual movements began which would flourish with the Renaissance. At the height of the wars a former wool merchant named William Caxton set up the first printing press in England, and soon printed books were helping to spread new ideas among the educated classes. Only five years after the Battle of Stoke Field in 1487 brought the wars to an end, Christopher Columbus would make his epic voyage to the New World, an event which profoundly altered the way that Europeans viewed the world. At the same time the feudal system had broken down. The Black Death a hundred years before had left a shortage of agricultural labourers. Peasants found that they could now demand high wages for their labour, and they refused to be tied to their lord's land. Towns were growing in importance, and a middle class made up of merchants, traders and prosperous yeoman farmers was emerging. This all helped make England a wealthier, more dynamic country, but it also made society more complex and harder to govern. Warfare was also changing: well-armed disciplined infantry had replaced the mounted knight in armour as the dominant force on the battlefield, and the widespread use of heavy cannon was rapidly making the traditional medieval castle obsolete. The Wars of the Roses occurred against this background of change and uncertainty, and reflect the determination of powerful noble families to retain their wealth and influence.

A modern visitor to St Albans might well assume that the Wars of the Roses are far removed from the present-day city, and that years of urban development will have swept away all traces of the old medieval town. However, such an assumption would be wrong. When we look more closely we see that the streets of central St Albans still follow the old medieval layout, and many of the original medieval buildings still exist. Almost uniquely for any medieval battlefield, we are able not only to follow the course of the action, but also to identify the exact locations where individual events occurred. We hope that anyone who reads this book will take the opportunity to walk in the footsteps of those Lancastrian and Yorkist soldiers who were prepared to fight and die for what they believed in five and a half centuries ago.

Chapter 1

THE DRIFT TO WAR

THE WARS OF THE ROSES are usually regarded as having begun with the First Battle of St Albans on 22 May 1455. However, the outbreak of serious fighting was the result of festering problems which had been poisoning the politics of medieval England for over sixty years. Many of the causes of the wars can be traced back to events that occurred in the previous century. King Edward III had fathered five sons, but his eldest son, Edward of Woodstock (the Black Prince), predeceased his father, dying in 1376. Therefore, when Edward III himself died in the summer of 1377 he was succeeded by his grandson, Richard II.

Richard II proved to be an unpopular king, vain, eccentric and capricious. The real power behind the throne was Richard's uncle, John of Gaunt, Duke of Lancaster, Edward III's third son. In 1399 Gaunt's eldest son, Henry Bolingbroke, led a successful rebellion against the king. Richard was forced to abdicate and was imprisoned in Pontefract Castle, where he was probably murdered the following year. Henry Bolingbroke was proclaimed King Henry IV, thus becoming the first of the 'Lancastrian' kings.

Henry IV was succeeded in 1413 by his eldest son, another Henry. Henry V was a brilliant soldier and is remembered as one of England's greatest warrior kings. One of Henry's first acts as king was to lay claim to the French throne and reopen the war with France. Ever since the Norman Conquest in 1066 the medieval kings of England had ruled extensive territories in France. In 1337, Edward III had laid claim to the French throne and began the conflict known as the Hundred Years War (1337–1453), though it would be more accurate to describe it as a series of wars which lasted for 116 years. Edward's claim was not unreasonable: on his mother's side he was the grandson of Philip IV of France. Edward and his son, the Black Prince, won a series of dramatic victories over the French but it became obvious to Edward that he did not have the resources to conquer the whole country. In 1360, therefore, Edward agreed to the Treaty of Bretigny, by which he gave up his claim to the throne of France in exchange for retaining all the territory he had gained. By the time Henry V decided to renew the war in 1415 the English controlled only Gascony and Calais. Henry V's campaigns were even more spectacularly successful than those of Edward III seventy years before. Henry's most famous victory was at the Battle of Agincourt in October 1415, when

Nineteenth-century engraving of Henry VI (from an original portrait at Eton College). Henry was England's most pious king but was swept up and captured in the fighting at both these battles and wounded in the first. *Peter Burley*

he decisively defeated a much larger French army. He was described by a contemporary as 'the most victorious, the invincible King'.

Within a few years Henry had conquered most of northern France. By the Treaty of Troyes in 1420, Henry agreed to marry Charles's daughter, Katherine of Valois, and in exchange was recognized by King Charles as Regent of France and rightful heir to the French throne. The treaty declared that Charles's son, the Dauphin Charles, was illegitimate and had no claim to the throne. However, two years later, Henry suddenly died of dysentery. Just two months after that King Charles followed him to the grave. We can never be certain, but it seems likely that if Henry V had lived for a few more years he would have succeeded in uniting the thrones of England and France, with far-reaching consequences for the course of European history. In the event, he was succeeded by his son, yet another Henry, only a few months old, who was now proclaimed Henry VI, rightful king of both England and France.

While Henry VI was only a child, power was in the hands of his two uncles: Humphrey, Duke of Gloucester, who was appointed Protector of the Realm and Chief Councillor, and John, Duke of Bedford, who was appointed Regent of France. French resistance to English rule had rallied round the disinherited dauphin, and in 1429 the tide turned. The French were inspired by a young peasant girl, Joan of Arc, who claimed that she was directed by spiritual 'voices' to save France. Led by Joan, the French army relieved the besieged City of Orleans, and then went on to capture Rheims, where the dauphin was solemnly crowned King Charles VII.

If the English fortunes in France were to be revived they desperately needed the leadership of a strong, warlike,

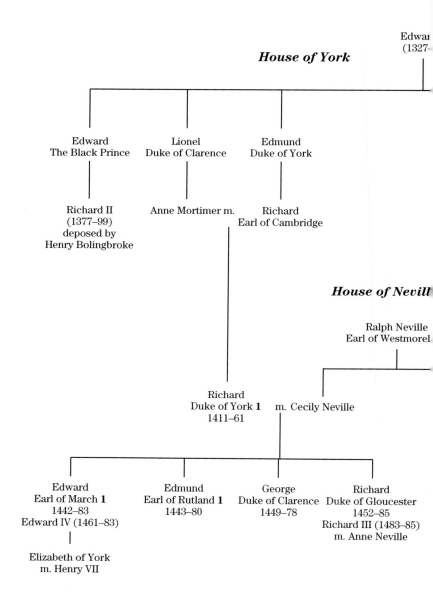

**Indicative Genealogy of the Royal
Houses.**

House of Lancaster

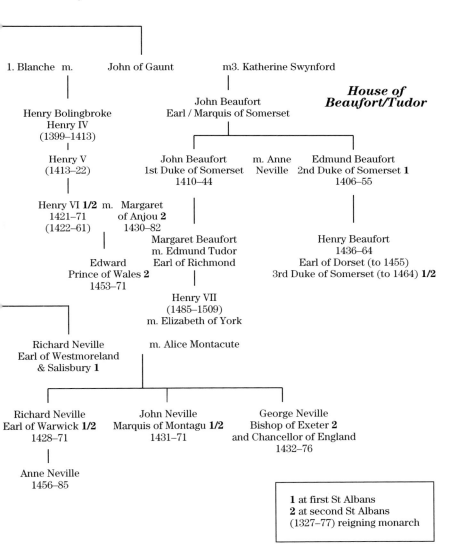

1. Blanche m.   John of Gaunt   m3. Katherine Swynford

John Beaufort
Earl / Marquis of Somerset

House of Beaufort/Tudor

Henry Bolingbroke
Henry IV
(1399–1413)

Henry V
(1413–22)

John Beaufort
1st Duke of Somerset
1410–44

m. Anne
Neville

Edmund Beaufort
2nd Duke of Somerset **1**
1406–55

Henry VI **1/2** m.   Margaret
1421–71   of Anjou **2**
(1422–61)   1430–82

Margaret Beaufort
m. Edmund Tudor
Earl of Richmond

Henry Beaufort
1436–64
Earl of Dorset (to 1455)
3rd Duke of Somerset (to 1464) **1/2**

Edward
Prince of Wales **2**
1453–71

Henry VII
(1485–1509)
m. Elizabeth of York

Richard Neville
Earl of Westmoreland
& Salisbury **1**

m. Alice Montacute

Richard Neville
Earl of Warwick **1/2**
1428–71

John Neville
Marquis of Montagu **1/2**
1431–71

George Neville
Bishop of Exeter **2**
and Chancellor of England
1432–76

Anne Neville
1456–85

1 at first St Albans
2 at second St Albans
(1327–77) reigning monarch

charismatic king like Henry V. Unfortunately, Henry VI was nothing like his father and proved completely unequal to the task. Henry was a deeply pious man who would spend long hours in prayer and reading the scriptures. According to his chaplain, 'His sole delight was to immerse himself day and night in the law of God.'

Such devotion may have delighted his chaplain, but did not impress the powerful noblemen around Henry, who could see that pressing matters of state were being badly neglected. Henry had little interest in conquest or in warfare and it is significant that his most lasting achievements were the founding of King's College at Eton and King's College at Cambridge. Although Henry may have been well intentioned he was also naïve, weak-willed, and simple-minded. As a result, all too often he was manipulated by corrupt and unscrupulous courtiers. A power struggle developed around Henry, with the Duke of Gloucester on one side and members of the powerful Beaufort family on the other. The Beauforts were descended from the illegitimate offspring of John of Gaunt and his mistress, Katherine Swynford. John of Gaunt had later married Katherine, making her his third wife, and their children had been legitimized by Act of Parliament.

The Beauforts and their chief ally, William de la Pole, Earl of Suffolk, were eager to end the costly and unsuccessful war in France. In 1444 Suffolk negotiated the Truce of Tours, by which King Henry was to marry Charles VII's niece Margaret of Anjou, and would retain Normandy and Aquitaine, but he agreed, in a secret clause to the treaty, to hand over Anjou and Maine to the French. The following year, sixteen-year-old Margaret of Anjou married Henry VI and thus became Queen of England. Margaret was beautiful, intelligent, strong-willed and high-spirited. Although Henry and Margaret were very different characters, the marriage appears to have been successful, and a genuine affection developed between them. In every other respect, however, the Truce of Tours was a dismal failure. The surrender of Anjou and Maine caused outrage and the agreement did not lead to a long-term peace as had been hoped, but resulted only in a short-term truce.

Suffolk became increasingly unpopular, with his main critic being Gloucester, who had always been a firm supporter of the war in France. In the spring of 1447, Henry arranged for Parliament to meet in Bury St Edmunds, but when Gloucester arrived he was promptly arrested. Within a few days Gloucester was dead and rumours quickly spread that he had been murdered on Suffolk's orders. There is no evidence for this and it is more likely that Gloucester died from either a stroke or a heart attack;

certainly he had led a debauched life for years and his arrest must have come as a shock. Suffolk gained nothing from Gloucester's death. If anything Gloucester proved to be more dangerous dead than he had been alive. His many faults were conveniently forgotten and he was remembered in popular folklore as the 'Good Duke Humphrey', a true patriot murdered on Suffolk's orders. Gloucester was eventually buried in St Albans Abbey, where his tomb can be seen to this day.

Gloucester's death helped push Richard, Duke of York into prominence as the next in line to the throne and, if Henry and Margaret failed to produce any children, quite possibly the next king. While Henry was the great-grandson of John of Gaunt, Richard was descended from Edward III's fourth son, Edmund, Duke of York. However, through his mother, Ann Mortimer, Richard could also claim descent from Edward III's second son, Lionel, Duke of Clarence. In the opinion of many this complicated family tree actually gave the Duke of York a stronger claim to the throne than King Henry himself. Not only did York have a strong claim to the throne, but he was also immensely wealthy in his own right, and controlled extensive lands in the Midlands, Wales and Ireland. York's marriage to Cecily Neville also meant that he was connected to one of the most powerful families in England. York's brother-in-law was Richard Neville, Earl of Salisbury, and

Humphrey of Gloucester was a key figure in the background to the Wars of the Roses. His is the only royal tomb in St Albans. *By kind permission of St Albans Abbey. Photograph: John Kliene*

Salisbury's son, another Richard Neville, was the Earl of Warwick in his own right and would eventually become better known to history as 'Warwick the Kingmaker'.

In 1436, York was appointed Lieutenant of France and for several years he struggled to retain the English possessions in France. A combination of incompetent financial management and lavish generosity of land and property to the king's favourites meant that the Crown was almost bankrupt and York frequently had to pay out from his own purse whenever the king failed to provide him with adequate funds. York must have felt that he received little appreciation for his efforts. In 1447 King Henry appointed York Lieutenant of Ireland and replaced him in France with Edmund Beaufort, Duke of Somerset. To add insult to injury, while the Crown was reluctant to pay York the money he was owed, generous funds were made available to Somerset. York also suspected that Somerset had ambitions to succeed to the throne. Although the Beauforts had been specifically excluded from the royal succession when they had been made legitimate, Somerset may well have reasoned that if one Act of Parliament could make the Beauforts John of Gaunt's legitimate heirs, then there was no reason why another Act could not make him heir to the throne ahead of York's claims. All this led to a bitter feud between the two

Richard Plantagenet, 3rd Duke of York (1411–60)

Richard, Duke of York enjoyed an undistinguished – but not unsuccessful – military career in France and then in Ireland, but his real interest was in gaining the throne for his House, not in battlefield glory.

He was alternately hesitant and impetuous, and this flaw showed up in his military as well as political performance. Over his lifetime he became steadily more of a risk-taker and by 1455 he had become 'an old man in a hurry'. He could also be arrogant and stubborn. He made both political and military misjudgements – leading to his failure to gain the throne in 1460 and then his own death at Wakefield later that year. He does appear to have been a personally brave leader and was in the thick of the fighting at St Albans in 1455.

men that would reach its bloody denouement eight years later in the streets of St Albans.

Somerset's period of office in France proved to be disastrous. In the summer of 1449 the French invaded Normandy. While the English garrisons in Normandy had been sadly neglected, the French had completely reorganized their army. The undisciplined French feudal levy had been replaced with a professional standing army, equipped with probably the finest artillery organization in the world at that time. The result was that English-held towns and castles fell in rapid succession. A small English army hurriedly scraped together and sent to Normandy was crushed at the Battle of Formigny in April 1450. By the end of the year the whole of Normandy had been lost.

The person who received most of the blame for the debacle in France was Suffolk, who had become one of the most unpopular men in England. Parliament moved to impeach him but, at the urging of the queen, Henry tried to save Suffolk's life by banishing him for five years. Suffolk took ship for the continent but was intercepted by a privateer vessel named *Nicholas of the Tower*. Suffolk was forcibly removed from his ship and placed in a small boat, where he was brutally beheaded. His body was

Edmund Beaufort, 2nd Duke of Somerset (1406–55)

Edmund Beaufort was the most experienced but the shortest lived of all the commanders in the two battles of St Albans, meeting his death only hours after the thirty years of conflict had started. His military career had started well enough in France in 1436, but he had suffered a series of reverses in later years and brought no greater acumen to St Albans than he had to Normandy. His only asset seemed to be his royal blood.

There is an intriguing legend about him that he would never enter a castle because he had been told he would be killed in one. If true, that must have been something of a handicap as a field commander.

The verdict on his generalship at St Albans must be that he invited the defeat – and his own death – by failing to prepare for the battle.

contemptuously thrown onto Dover beach and his head stuck on a stake.

Worse was to follow: a full-scale rebellion broke out in Kent led by a local landowner named Jack Cade. The rebels had a clear agenda – they wanted the councillors around King Henry removed and York returned from Ireland. King Henry proved to be incapable of dealing with the rebellion effectively and fled to Kenilworth Castle. For a while the rebels even had control of London itself. Eventually the rebellion collapsed and Cade was fatally wounded resisting arrest, but the rebellion had brutally demonstrated the weakness and impotence of Henry VI's government. For the first time in over a generation Englishmen had fought each other on English soil, and Cade's rebellion was to prove to be a mere curtain-raiser for the turmoil to come.

In September 1450, York returned from Ireland. He was concerned about rumours which were being circulated accusing him of being one of the instigators of Cade's rebellion. He was also anxious to have Somerset removed from office and himself declared the rightful heir to the throne. Despairing of achieving his aims by peaceful means, in February 1452 York gathered his supporters and raised an armed rebellion. Unfortunately for York, he received much less support than he had been hoping for. Although many noblemen were sympathetic to York's position, they were very reluctant to take up arms against their lawful king. At Blackheath, York negotiated with the king and agreed to disband his army on the understanding that Somerset would be arrested and brought to trial. However, far from being arrested Somerset continued to act as the king's chief adviser, while York himself was treated as if he was a defeated rebel. When the king and Somerset returned to London, York had to ride in front of them, as if he was their prisoner. York then had to swear a solemn oath, in public, at St Paul's Cathedral that he would never again take up arms against the king. For the next eighteen months York retired to his estates in the north to brood on his humiliating failure and the way in which he believed he had been tricked.

Somerset may have been able to deal with the threat from York, but he could do little to retrieve the deteriorating situation in France. By 1453 the French had invaded the province of Gascony. The Gascons had been ruled by the English Crown for over 300 years. English rule was popular and the Gascons were deeply suspicious of the French king's ambitions. Soon urgent appeals for help were being received in London as the Gascons tried to resist the French invasion. An English army was hastily assembled and despatched under the command of Sir John Talbot, Earl of

Shrewsbury. Sir John was a tough old veteran of the French Wars and although he was almost seventy years old the French still feared and respected him. The decisive battle was fought in July 1453, when Talbot tried to relieve the besieged town of Castillon by attacking the French encampment. The French camp was strongly fortified and the French artillery played havoc with the attacking English and Gascon columns. When the French counter-attacked the Anglo-Gascon army was routed. Talbot was among the slain. Castillon was the last major battle of the Hundred Years War. By the autumn of 1453 the whole of Gascony had been lost. Of all the lands in France that Henry VI had inherited from his father, only the city of Calais and the surrounding County of Guines still remained an English possession.

King Henry was at his hunting lodge at Clarendon in Wiltshire when the terrible news of Castillon arrived. The disaster in Gascony had a devastating effect on Henry, who suffered a complete mental collapse. Although we cannot be certain from this distance, it seems probable that Henry suffered from some form of hysterical catatonia. It also seems likely that he may have inherited this mental illness from his maternal grandfather, King Charles VI. Henry's mind withdrew into a twilight world where he seemed to be oblivious of everything going on around him. If food was put in front of him he would eat, or if he was put to bed he would sleep, but most of the time he would simply stare into space, seemingly incapable of recognizing the people around him or of responding to any conversation. Just two months later, in October 1453, Margaret gave birth to a son, Edward of Lancaster, Prince of Wales, who now became heir to the throne. The arrival of Prince Edward meant, of course, that the dispute between York and Somerset as to who was the rightful heir had now become irrelevant. Unfortunately, given the state of the king's health, dangerous rumours soon spread that Henry might not be the young Prince Edward's real father. No evidence has ever been found to support this theory, but inevitably the rumours were highly damaging. With the birth of her son, Margaret appears to have become obsessed with the idea that York posed a major threat to Prince Edward ever succeeding to the throne. Margaret was determined to find a way to curtail the power and influence of York. With the country reeling from the news of the defeat in France and King Henry clearly incapable of ruling the country, it was a highly dangerous and volatile situation.

In October, Queen Margaret and Somerset suggested to the Great Council that they should jointly be given the regency and govern the country until the king recovered from his illness. The Council was not impressed and quickly rejected this proposal.

The following month the Council went further. John Mowbray, Duke of Norfolk, accused Somerset of corruption and being responsible for 'the loss of two so noble Duchies as Normandy and Guyenne'. Somerset was arrested and put in the Tower. A Commission of Inquiry was ordered to investigate Somerset's handling of affairs in France. Margaret must have realized with dismay that with Henry's illness power was slipping away from her, and York, in disgrace just eighteen months before, was now being seen as the possible saviour of the country.

In March 1454, Parliament voted to appoint York as Protector and Defender of the Realm. It was none too soon. The country desperately needed a firm government. The lack of a strong central authority meant that in some country areas powerful noblemen were taking the law into their own hands. This was particularly so in the north, where the rivalry between the Percys and the Nevilles had degenerated into almost open warfare. York, in his new role as Protector of the Realm, energetically set about tackling the biggest problems facing the country. First, he had to bring the royal finances under control. Second, he had to deal with those turbulent barons who thought that they were above the law. Within a few months great progress had been made, but much still remained to be done, when, during the Christmas of 1454, the whole political situation was turned upside down. Just as suddenly as Henry had suffered his mental collapse, he suddenly recovered. He had no memory of anything that had happened during the previous seventeen months:

> He asked what the Prince's name was, and the Queen told
> him Edward; and then he held up his hands and thanked God
> thereof. And he said he never knew till that time, nor wist
> what was said to him, nor wist not where he had been, whilst
> he had been sick, till now.

It has been said of Henry that his mental illness was a personal tragedy but his recovery was a national disaster; it provided the spark that finally ignited the Wars of the Roses. Margaret wasted no time in persuading Henry that Somerset should be released from the Tower and restored to office. Early in February 1455, Somerset emerged from the Tower complaining bitterly that he had been held a prisoner for over a year without any formal charges ever being brought against him. Somerset was restored to the offices of Constable of England and Captain of Calais; he was once more the king's chief adviser. The Commission of Inquiry to investigate the loss of Normandy and Gascony was quietly dropped. A few days later Henry was well enough to address

Parliament and thank the members for their loyalty and concern. He then accepted York's resignation from his position as Protector of the Realm. In the next few weeks Salisbury, John Tiptoft, Earl of Worcester and the rest of York's allies were all dismissed from office. For the Yorkists it was incredibly frustrating – they had been given a taste of power for a few months only to see it snatched away from them and given to Somerset, a man whom they utterly despised. It was not just the loss of power that concerned York and his allies; it began to be increasingly obvious that Margaret and Somerset intended to crush and humble the Yorkists so that they could never be a threat again. The Yorkist leaders feared that their property, their freedom and possibly even their lives were in danger.

In April, Somerset and his allies held a conference in Westminster. Significantly, neither York, Salisbury nor any of their friends were invited to attend. The conference resolved to call a Great Council in May, at Leicester. Summonses were sent out to all the leading noblemen, ordering them to attend the king at Leicester on 21 May. The purpose of the Council was ominously described as 'To provide for the Kings safety against his enemies'.

The wording of the summons outraged the Yorkists. They were already deeply suspicious about the conference, to which they had not been invited, and now they demanded to know who were these supposed enemies of the king. As they stated, the phrase 'of common presumption implieth a mistrust of some persons'.

As the Council was never held we cannot be certain what Somerset was planning, but it seems likely that Somerset intended to have York arrested and put on trial. It also seems likely that the main reason for holding the Council in Leicester rather than London was because York was too popular in London and it would be much easier to deal with him in Leicester, where he would have few supporters. To York the whole situation must have seemed all too reminiscent of that in 1447 when Gloucester had been called to attend a Parliament in Bury St Edmunds, and York had no intention of sharing Gloucester's fate. He, Salisbury and Warwick quietly left London and retired to their estates in the north. York went to Sandal Castle, Salisbury to Middleham Castle, and Warwick to Warwick Castle.

At some point during April or early May the momentous decision was made that Somerset would have to be removed by force of arms. York had learned from the fiasco of his abortive rebellion three years before the importance of co-ordinating his actions with his allies. During the early weeks of May, hard-riding messengers were criss-crossing the Midlands keeping the leading Yorkists in touch with each other. At the same time, other messengers were calling on their friends, tenants and retainers to assemble and support their lord. Swords, axes, spears and bills were being sharpened, and as hundreds of armed men gathered, Sandal, Warwick and Middleham were turned into armed camps. A political crisis had become a military confrontation and England was sliding inexorably towards civil war.

Chapter 2

THE FIRST BATTLE OF ST ALBANS

BY THE MIDDLE OF MAY 1455 the political crisis, which had been steadily growing ever since King Henry's unexpected recovery in December 1454, had reached breaking point. While the Duke of Somerset and his allies were still plotting how to politically outmanoeuvre the Yorkists, the Duke of York and the Nevilles had decided that they had no choice but to resort to the threat of force of arms in order to remove Somerset from office. By the middle of May the Yorkists had raised an army and were marching on London down the old Roman road of Ermine Street.

With York were his two most important allies: Richard Neville, Earl of Salisbury, and Salisbury's son, Richard Neville, Earl of Warwick. York was also accompanied by his two eldest sons, thirteen-year-old Edward, Earl of March, who was getting his first experience of campaigning, and twelve-year-old Edmund, Earl of Rutland. Little could Warwick have realized that in the years to come the Earl of March would be both his most important ally and ultimately his deadliest enemy. York was hoping to be joined by Ralph, Lord Cromwell, and John Mowbray, Duke of Norfolk, who was raising a force of men. In fact they did not join the rebel army until 23 May, the day after the First Battle of St Albans. There may have been good reasons for Norfolk's tardiness, but it is also likely

---

Richard Neville, 5th Earl of Salisbury and Earl of Westmoreland (1400–60)

Salisbury had never played much of a military role, despite his age and seniority. His role at St Albans in 1455 was to lead one of the frontal attacks on the Bars, where he was in the thick of the fighting. His moment of glory was in 1460 when he became the only commander ever to invest and force the surrender of the Tower of London. Later that year, though, Somerset comprehensively outwitted the Yorkists at Wakefield and York and Salisbury were killed.

The Bear and Ragged Staff badge of the Earl of Warwick (here shown as a decoration on a pub in Tewkesbury), who was to be blooded for the first time in the First Battle of St Albans. *Steve Goodchild*

that he was deliberately being cautious and was reluctant to involve himself too deeply with the rebellion until he was confident of its success.

There has been much interest among historians about the number of peers who supported the Yorkist cause. As a group the majority of peers were predominantly and consistently Lancastrian and the only peers definitely with York on 22 May were Salisbury, Warwick, Lord Clinton and Lord Cobham. One of the immediate fall-outs from the battle was the number of peers who claimed to have been en route to support York, but somehow just missed the actual battle.

Unaware of the Yorkists' preparations for war, Somerset sent a delegation north to negotiate with York and the Nevilles. Presumably the intention was to persuade them to attend the Great Council at Leicester, and it is likely that promises were made guaranteeing their safety. This delegation consisted of Reynold Boulers, Bishop of Coventry, John Tiptoft, Earl of Worcester, and Robert Botyll, Prior of the Hospital of St John of Jerusalem. However, their mission had little or no chance of success: York and the Nevilles did not trust Somerset and were prepared to defend themselves with force. According to one contemporary account the delegation was detained so that they could give no warning to the king or Somerset while the Yorkist army marched on London.

It was only on 18 May that definite news arrived in London that the Yorkists had raised and armed their retainers and were marching south. Suddenly all of Somerset's plans were disrupted and the Great Council at Leicester, which was due to be held on the 21st, had to be postponed. Messages were hastily sent to those peers whose loyalty King Henry could rely on, ordering them to raise men and join him as quickly as possible. However, the Yorkists had achieved a strategic surprise and it was unlikely that sufficient loyal troops could be raised to confront them before they reached London. For example, on 18 May a message was sent to Coventry demanding that a force of men be immediately

Richard Neville, Earl of Warwick ('Warwick the Kingmaker') (1428–71)

Warwick, 'the last of the barons', was the main protagonist at both battles and we need to understand why his performance was so different at each.

St Albans 1455 was his first battle, aged twenty-six, and he showed himself immediately to be a charismatic man who led from the front and never shirked a challenge. The situation half an hour into the battle played to his strengths of taking action against the odds and seizing the moment.

Fatal flaws, however, led to defeat at St Albans in 1461 and death at Barnet in 1471. He hesitated when faced with complexity and he had trouble grasping the larger picture. The situation in February 1461 showed up all his weaknesses, in that he dithered, then misjudged, and then reinforced his own failure on the battlefield.

He was also beguiled by the tactic of the artillery ambush, but failed to see its limitations. This led him to make rigid and inappropriate deployments at St Albans in 1461, where he managed to pull his irons out of the fire, and at Barnet, where he did not.

Warwick had a particular quirk in his battlefield command. He always fought on foot in the vanguard of the troops he was leading. This made him an inspiring leader to the men around him, but he lost mobility and the ability to see all that was happening. It served him well in 1455, but it may have been one of the things that cost him the battle in 1461 and it certainly cost him his life at Barnet.

He was an inspired subaltern but a disastrous general.

assembled in the king's service, 'to be with us wheresoever we be in all haste possible'. The Council at Coventry resolved that a force 'be made ready in all haste possible to go to our Sovereign Lord to St Albans and to abide with him and to do him service'. Unfortunately for Somerset, the Battle of St Albans had already been fought and the issue had been decided before these men had even left Coventry. A number of peers loyal to the king did in fact arrive in St Albans, with their retinues, on Friday 23, but they were twenty-four hours too late to affect the outcome of the battle.

As well as trying to raise a loyal army, Somerset instructed the Chancellor, Thomas Bourchier, Archbishop of Canterbury, to send letters to York, Salisbury, Warwick and the Duke of Norfolk informing them of the king's displeasure at their actions in raising an army, and ordering them to immediately disband their forces, each of them being allowed to retain only a personal retinue. York, Salisbury and Warwick were at Royston and on 20 May sent a letter to the Chancellor in reply. In the letter they insisted that they were loyal to the king and had raised an armed force 'only to keep ourselves out of the danger whereunto our enemies have not ceased to study, labour and compass to bring us'. They were suspicious of the fact that they had not been invited to the conference at Westminster in mid-April, and questioned the wording of the invitation to the Great Council at Leicester, with its suggestion that the king needed to be safeguarded against his enemies. Who were these enemies supposed to be, the Yorkists asked? The real problem for York and the Nevilles, although they could not say this in the letter, was that they were convinced that Henry's feeble mind was being poisoned against them by Somerset. They firmly believed that Somerset, in collaboration with the queen, had told the king that they were traitors who would have to be dealt with, and they believed that if they attended the Council at Leicester they risked sharing the same fate as that which had befallen Humphrey, Duke of Gloucester at Bury St Edmunds in 1447. The Yorkists were determined that it was Somerset who should be removed from office, arrested and put on trial.

Meanwhile, Somerset had realized that it would be disastrous to try and confront York and the Nevilles in pro-Yorkist London, so on 21 May Somerset and the king left Westminster. The intention was to rendezvous with loyal forces at St Albans, and proceed slowly on towards Leicester, collecting reinforcements on the way. The king was accompanied by Somerset together with his eldest son, the Earl of Dorset, and the Duke of Buckingham, together with his eldest son, the Earl of Stafford. There were four other earls: the Earl of Northumberland, the Earl of Pembroke, the Earl of Devon, and the Earl of Wiltshire. There were also five barons: Lords Roos, Sudeley, Clifford, Fauconberg and Dudley. Only the absence of Queen Margaret and the young Prince of Wales, both of whom had been sent to Greenwich for safety, indicated that this was meant to be an army on the march, not a Royal Court making a stately progress through a peaceful countryside.

The royal party had only reached Kilburn, some four miles from Westminster, when, at 10 a.m., they were overtaken by John Say, Keeper of the Privy Palace at Westminster, carrying the Yorkists' letter. According to later Yorkist accounts, Somerset conspired with two of the king's servants, Thomas Thorpe and William Joseph, to prevent the king from seeing the contents of the letter. However, this version of events has to be treated with some caution, for after the battle the Yorkists were eager to put all the blame for the conflict onto Somerset. Whether the king saw the letter or not, it appears to have made no difference to the royal party's plans – they pushed on and by the evening they were sixteen miles from Westminster and had reached Watford, where they halted for the night. At the same time the Yorkists were marching the sixteen miles from Royston to Ware. At Ware they wrote a second letter, repeating much of what had already been conveyed in the first letter, but this time it was addressed directly to King Henry himself. The letter was taken by William Willeflete, confessor to the Duke of York, and handed to the Earl of Devon at 2 a.m. on Thursday, 22 May. According to Yorkist accounts, this second letter suffered the same fate as the first one, with Somerset, Thorpe and Joseph conspiring to make sure that the king never actually saw the letter's contents. However, the arrival of this messenger in the middle of the night must have emphasized that the situation was becoming desperately urgent and time was rapidly running out. The Lancastrians decided to press on to St Albans with all speed. Early the next morning messengers warned Henry and Somerset that the Yorkists were no longer advancing on London; instead they were marching to intercept the king at St Albans and they could be expected to reach there at the same time as the royal army. The distance from Watford to St Albans is only some eight miles, compared to a distance of seventeen miles from Ware to St Albans, so the Yorkists had made remarkably good time. It seems likely that the Yorkists had only stayed briefly in Ware the previous day before pushing on towards St Albans. They had probably camped overnight, at some unknown spot, somewhere on the road between Ware and St Albans. Once again the Yorkists had successfully seized the strategic initiative and placed Somerset and the king in a dilemma. Somerset must have been aware that although reinforcements were expected they were unlikely to arrive before the following day at the earliest. In the meantime, the small royal army was outnumbered and ill-prepared for battle. Although it contained many experienced commanders it was far too small in overall numbers, only totalling between 2,000 and 2,500 men. Most of the army was made up of the various peers' personal retinues, reinforced by a few levies from East Anglia. The royal army appears to have been particularly short of archers, and the longbow was one of the decisive weapons of fifteenth-century English warfare.

There are various estimates of the size of the Yorkist army, with some contemporary chroniclers claiming that York had 5,000, or even 7,000 men with him. However, these figures are almost certainly an exaggeration. Considering that Norfolk had not yet joined them, it is unlikely that the Yorkists had more than 3,000 men present. However, this still gave them a clear numerical advantage, and, more important than mere numbers, the Yorkists appear to have been much better prepared for battle. Their army included a contingent of 600 archers from the Scottish Marches

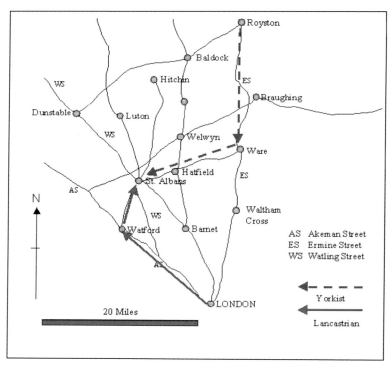

Map 1. The First Battle of St Albans – the approach marches.

under the command of an experienced soldier, Sir Robert Ogle. These men were to play a crucial role in the forthcoming battle.

When King Henry became aware of the proximity of the Yorkist army there was a crucial roadside conference. The question was whether the royal party should march to St Albans, confront the Yorkists, and try to achieve some sort of compromise through negotiation without the need for bloodshed. The alternative was to halt where they were, prepare for battle, and await the expected reinforcements which would enable them to crush the Yorkists once and for all. It would be wrong to assume that all the noblemen accompanying the king were loyal allies of Somerset. In fact Somerset could probably rely on the wholehearted support only of his son, the Earl of Dorset, James Butler, Earl of Wiltshire, the Earl of Northumberland and Thomas, Lord Clifford. Northumberland's and Clifford's support could be relied on because of their bitter rivalry with the Nevilles. Many of the other noblemen were present only because of their loyalty to the king and they had little desire to find themselves caught up in a battle between York and Somerset. The Earl of Devon, for example, had been one of the few peers who had supported York in his abortive rebellion in 1452, while William Neville, Baron Fauconberg was Salisbury's half-brother.

Buckingham strongly urged the king to proceed to St Albans and settle the matter through negotiation. Buckingham was convinced that York would be willing to reach a compromise as he had done at Blackheath in 1452. Somerset must have bitterly regretted that Queen Margaret was not present to support his argument. Instead, for once he found Henry unwilling to listen. Henry overruled Somerset, appointed Buckingham Constable of England, and put him in charge of the negotiations. The royal party then proceeded on their way to St Albans. It proved to be a fateful decision.

The royal army reached St Albans early on the morning of the 22nd, probably about 7 a.m., although various times between 4 a.m. and 9 a.m. have been suggested. Unfortunately, in the Middle Ages people were rarely able to be precise about time and distance, and we cannot be more certain about the time of Henry's arrival. The Lancastrians entered the town from the south-west, marching up Holywell Hill and into St Peter's Street. In 1455 the modern Chequer Street had not yet been named and this stretch of road up to Shropshire Lane was still part of Holywell Hill. The king had visited St Albans before and usually stayed in the Abbey. However, on this occasion, with the Yorkist army so near, Henry went to the house of Edmund Westby, a prominent St Albans citizen. The exact location of the house is uncertain, but it is presumed to have been near the Market Place and close to the

Thomas Clifford (of Craven), 8th Baron Clifford (1414–55)

Thomas Clifford is Shakespeare's 'Clifford of Cumberland', who was tasked with leading the defence of the Sopwell Lane Bar against York's attack in 1455. He had a reputation as an efficient organizer in the Scottish Border wars and a personally brave fighter. He is credited in Shakespeare with killing York's horse during the close fighting there. He was killed when the Lancastrian position collapsed.

centre of the town. The royal army made the Moot Hall their head-quarters. As explained in a later chapter, St Albans was not a walled town, though there was a ditch around the town, called the Tonman Ditch. Behind the ditch there was a rampart surmounted variously by some sort of hedge, fence or palisade along its length. The buildings backing onto the ditch were known as the 'town backsides'. Three roads crossed the ditch and entered St Albans from the east: these were Cock Lane (now called Hatfield Road), Shropshire Lane (now called Victoria Street), and Sopwell Lane. The reader should note that the modern London Road did not then exist. Thick wooden beams or 'Bars' could be quickly dragged across to block these roads. As soon as the Lancastrians had occupied the centre of the town, orders were given to man the Bars and the fence in case of a Yorkist attack. Lord Clifford, an experienced soldier, was put in charge of these defences. He was assisted by commanders such as Sir Bertine Entwistle and Sir Richard Harrington, both veterans of the French Wars. According to Benet, 'The town was strongly barred and arrayed for defence.'

The Yorkist army appears to have arrived at St Albans either at the same time as the royal army, or very shortly afterwards. Their approach from Ware would have taken them along Hatfield Road, which became Cock Lane as it entered the town at St Peter's Green. They did not, however, press on down Cock Lane but turned south at some point to set up camp to the east of the town in Keyfield, 'within range of a crossbow from the town'. It is tempting to speculate that the turn they took was to march along the bottom of the Tonman Ditch, which was an archery butts-cum-roadway here, thus incidentally allowing them to survey the town's defences. It has been suggested that the Yorkists actually arrived first, but this is not confirmed by contemporary accounts, and if the Yorkists did arrive first it seems curious that they did not seize the opportunity to occupy the town.

The arrival of the two armies was followed by some three hours of negotiations, 'without any stroke smitten on either party'. Such an occurrence was not uncommon, particularly during the early years of the Wars of the Roses, when there were still many people on both sides hopeful of resolving issues through negotiation rather than violence. Negotiations had previously managed to prevent a battle at Blackheath in 1452, and were to do so again at Ludlow in 1459. However, as the wars continued both sides became increasingly ruthless, and such attempts at restraint became rare.

The negotiations were conducted by heralds, who were sent between the leading figures on both sides. According to the Dijon Relation, 'The 22nd day of the said month very early the King sent a herald to the Duke of York to know the cause for which he had come there with so many men.' The Yorkists protested their loyalty to the king but insisted that Somerset be arrested and handed over to them, presumably to be put on trial. York's message to the king was uncompromising: 'We shall not now cease

Chequer Street, from London Road towards the location of the Queen's Hotel. *Mike Elliott*

Keyfield: the Yorkist assembly area with the earth rampart behind the Tonman Ditch marked by the wall on the right. *Mike Elliott*

… until we have them which have deserved death or else we die therefore.'

Buckingham tried to convince York that he was not there as Somerset's ally, but only as a loyal subject of the king:

> We wish the whole world to know that we have not come here to support any one person or for any other cause but only to be in company with the King our said Lord as by right we are bound to do.

But it must have become increasingly obvious to Buckingham that he had misjudged the situation. York was determined not to be deceived by vague promises, as he felt that he had been duped at Blackheath three years earlier. At the same time it must have been obvious, even to the naïve and unworldly Henry, that to give in to threats of violence and surrender a royal duke to the rebels would be to abdicate any pretence of royal authority. Both sides were also probably aware that the Yorkists currently had the advantage of numbers, but reinforcements of loyal troops were expected in St Albans in a day or so and the balance of numbers could quickly shift in favour of the Lancastrians. Certainly Buckingham appears to have tried to play for time, at one stage suggesting to the Yorkists that they ease the tension by withdrawing their army to Hatfield or Barnet for the night while they awaited some ecclesiastics to arrive to help with the negotiations.

When it became increasingly obvious that a compromise was unlikely to be reached, attitudes began to harden on both sides. The Yorkists were told to quit the field or face total forfeiture, and the Royal Standard was raised. This was an important symbolic moment and its significance was clearly understood by both sides – as it would be again when Charles I raised the Royal Standard in Nottingham in 1642 to initiate the Civil War. It meant that the King of England was prepared to go to war with any rebels and traitors present. All loyal subjects were required to either support the king, or immediately quit the field. Failure to do so could result in the individuals concerned being labelled traitors, their lands being forfeit and their heirs disinherited. It is not certain at what point in the negotiations the Royal Standard was raised. The Stowe Relation appears to suggest that it was raised shortly after the royal army arrived at St Albans, but the Stowe Relation is biased in favour of the Yorkists and tries to portray the king as being unreasonable, leaving York with no option but to fight. By comparison, the Fastolf Relation suggests that the Royal Standard was raised only when it became clear that the negotiations were not going to succeed. According to the Stowe Relation, the Royal Standard was raised in St Peter's Street near a place called 'Goselowe', and afterwards known as 'Sandeforthe'. It has not been possible to locate exactly where Goselowe or Sandeforthe was situated, but it must have been close to the old Town Hall, probably near the present-day Boots store!

The Stowe Relation also claims that King Henry sent a threatening and uncompromising message to the Yorkist leadership:

> I, King Harry, charge and command that no manner of persons of whatever degree or state abide not but void the field and be not so hardy as to make any resistance against me in my own realm for I shall know what traitors dare to be so bold as to raise the people in my own land, where-through I am in great disease and heaviness, and by the faith that I owe to St Edward and to the Crown of England, I shall destroy them every mother's son, and they shall be hanged, drawn and quartered that may be taken afterward. Rather than they shall have any Lord here with me at this time, I shall this day, for their sake and in this quarrel, myself live or die!

This stern reply seems out of character for the normally peaceful and pious Henry. One possibility is that it was an unexpected and petulant intervention by Henry himself, and this would explain why events suddenly moved faster than the Lancastrian commanders had anticipated. It is also possible that it was a subsequent forgery included in the Stowe Relation to help justify the Yorkists' actions, but whether the king uttered these words or not, it had become obvious that the issue could not now be resolved by negotiation. Three times York had sent his messenger, Mowbray Herald, into the town to demand Somerset's surrender. When he returned the third time he found that the Yorkists had their armour on and their banners unfurled, and they were forming up to attack. The heavily armoured knights and men-at-arms were preceded by the archers, who unleashed volleys of arrows on the hapless defenders of the Bars. York led a column of men up Shropshire Lane while Salisbury advanced up Sopwell Lane to attack the Bars, which had been hurriedly barricaded and were fiercely defended.

Inside the town this sudden attack caused pandemonium. As negotiations had dragged on it had been assumed that somehow a peaceful settlement would be reached. Many of the defenders had slipped away from their posts looking for food and drink. Most of the peers were still with the king and few had bothered to put on their elaborate full suits of plate armour. As the Yorkist attack began the alarm rang out loudly from the curfew bell in the Clock Tower, groups of defenders hurriedly ran back to their posts, and in the centre of the town knights and noblemen were frantically shouting for their servants to help them don their suits of armour. Within the Abbey monks and clergy fell to their knees and desperately prayed to the Blessed St Alban to intervene and save them from the ravages of war. The bewildered and frightened townsfolk could do little but barricade themselves in their homes, helpless victims of a quarrel that was not of their making. It was 10 o'clock on the morning of Thursday, 22 May 1455, and the Wars of the Roses had begun.

Both the Yorkist columns encountered

The Clock Tower, built 1403–12. *Mike Elliott*

determined resistance at the Bars and soon fierce hand-to-hand fighting was raging across the barriers in both Shropshire Lane and Sopwell Lane. In both locations the narrow lanes meant that the Yorkists were unable to deploy their men effectively and take advantage of their superior numbers and archers. As the minutes passed with neither York nor Salisbury able to break through the barriers, the situation began to look increasingly desperate for the Yorkist cause. However, the course of the battle was dramatically altered by the intervention of the Earl of Warwick. Only twenty-six years old, Warwick's role appears to have been to command a force of reserves situated halfway between York's and Salisbury's columns. Warwick was accompanied by Sir Robert Ogle, an experienced soldier who, it will be recalled, was in command of 600 archers. We cannot be sure whether it was Warwick who instinctively realized what needed to be done, or if he was advised by the more experienced Ogle, but somebody on the Yorkist side realized that there was no point in trying to reinforce either York's or Salisbury's columns, both of which were involved in a confused mêlée at the Bars. What was needed was a determined attack on the weakly defended sector halfway between Sopwell Lane and Shropshire Lane. The length of the ditch on the east side of St Albans was approximately 1,000 yards. Considering that the Lancastrian army was only just over 2,000 men, and most of those were either at the Bars or with the king in the centre of the town, it is obvious that the rest of the fence and ditch could only have

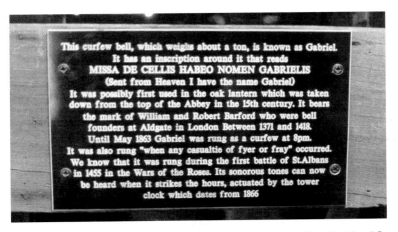

'Gabriel', the bell in the Clock Tower, was rung during the First Battle of St Albans. It now strikes the hours. *Mike Elliott*

29

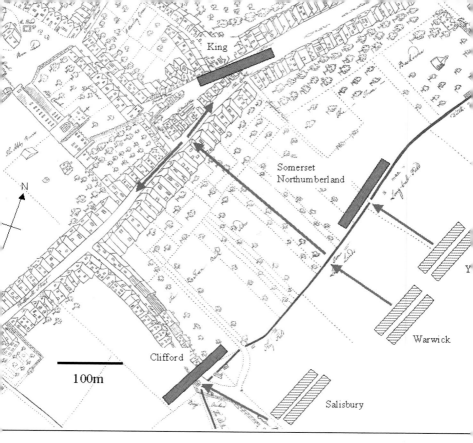

Map 2. The First Battle of St Albans. The deployment is shown on the 1634
Benjamin Hare map. The troop dispositions are conjectural, but the
frontages are correct. Each block is four ranks deep.

been manned by a thin screen of defenders, if at all. Given their
relative lack of manpower, the Lancastrians could only have
afforded to deploy defenders in numbers to where they knew the
Yorkists to be. There could have been no question of covering all
the eastern approaches. Likewise, the initial Yorkist attack had
showed no finesse and was a frontal attack taking the most
obvious routes. Warwick's attack was quickly organized, a volley
of arrows from the Yorkist archers kept the defenders occupied,
and this was followed by a determined assault by Warwick's men,
who stormed over the ditch and rampart and on through the fence.
The Tonman Ditch lay some 250 yards from Holywell Hill and St
Peter's Street. Holywell Hill itself was lined with shops, houses

and inns, built to cater for the needs of the numerous pilgrims who flocked to St Albans from all over England. However, between Holywell Hill and the ditch there were few substantial buildings. Most of this area appears to have been covered with a mixture of orchards, vegetable gardens and outbuildings, such as stables, sheds and barns. These would have provided few serious obstacles to Warwick's men, who swept forward, finding their way round the outbuildings and simply demolishing any fences that were in their way. Eventually Warwick's men burst into Holywell Hill at a point between two inns, the Key and the Chequer, shouting 'A Warwick, a Warwick!', and waving the Warwick banner of 'the bear and ragged staff'. The Stowe Relation describes the scene:

> They ferociously broke in by the garden sides between the sign of The Key and the sign of The Chequer in Holywell Street, and immediately they were within the town, suddenly they blew up trumpets, and set a cry with a shout and a great voice 'A Warwick! A Warwick!'

The English Chronicle is equally dramatic, though less precise about the exact location: 'They and their men violently broke down houses and fences on the East side of the town and entered St Peter's street, slaying all that resisted them.'

As Warwick's men spread out, turning both left and right, up and down Holywell Hill, the gallant defenders of the barriers, who had been putting up such determined resistance, now found themselves outflanked and threatened with attack from both front and rear. They fell back in confusion, hoping to join the remainder of the Lancastrian army in the centre of

A longbow man preparing to shoot. Ogle's 600 archers started the destruction of the Lancastrian army.
John Kliene

View from Maltings Car Park – the line of Warwick's attack. *Mike Elliott*

the town, but it is doubtful if many succeeded. It was probably at this stage of the battle that Lord Clifford, and many of his commanders, such as Sir Bertine Entwistle and Sir Richard Harrington, were killed. Sir Bertine was a distinguished veteran of the French Wars who came from the village of Entwistle, near Turton, in Lancashire. Another noble family who suffered in the battle were the Babthorpes from Hemingbrough, near Selby, in Yorkshire. Sir Ralph Babthorpe was accompanied by his son, also named Ralph Babthorpe, who was acting as his squire; tragically, both father and son were killed in the fighting. Entwistle and both the Babthorpes were buried in St Peter's Church at the north end of the town.

With the Yorkists storming into the town at three different points, the remaining Lancastrian noblemen, together with their personal retainers and members of the king's household, rallied around the king and the Royal Standard at the southern end of St Peter's Street, a fine broad thoroughfare usually used as the cattle market. So fast had been Warwick's advance that many of the Lancastrian noblemen had still not completed putting on their armour. The men around the king made an easy target for the Yorkist archers and soon a veritable storm of arrows swept across the market place. Within a few minutes many of the king's household had been killed around him and King Henry himself had been slightly wounded. The Dijon Relation describes the scene:

Sir Robert Ogle (later 1st Baron Ogle) (1406–69)

Sir Robert Ogle was a professional soldier, allied to the Nevilles, who brought 600 men from the Borders in 1455. He is credited with the realization that the Lancastrian position in the first battle was vulnerable to attack through the gardens backing on to the Tonman Ditch between the Lancastrian strong points.

He is not recorded at any other battles until Towton, and was created Baron Ogle in 1461 in recognition of his services as the principal Yorkist supporter in Northumberland. Alone among all the commanders at the first battle, he died peacefully (in 1469).

Looking north from the top of the Clock Tower. *Mike Elliott*

Matters became so critical that four of the King's bodyguard were killed by arrows in his presence, and the King himself was wounded in the shoulder by an arrow, although it only grazed the skin.

As the triumphant Yorkists swept forward there was little organized resistance. The Royal Standard was abandoned and thrown to the ground. The feeble way that the standard had been defended was regarded by many as disgraceful. Under warrior kings such as Edward III or Henry V the mere sight of the Royal Standard of England was enough to inspire feelings of dread in foreign foes and domestic rebels alike, but now the standard was found propped against the end of a house and was contemptuously thrown down on the ground. Contemporary accounts disagree as to who was responsible for this disgrace, but Sir Philip Wentworth, Lord Sudeley and Wiltshire are variously accused of being responsible for the standard and failing to do their duty.

The Market Place was strewn with dead and dying men. Somewhere among the carnage lay the body of the Neville's great rival, Henry Percy, Earl of Northumberland. Abbot John Whethamstede was an eyewitness and later described the scene

The modern street scene of the view seen in Graham Turner's painting of the first battle. (See colour plate section.) *Mike Elliott*

Henry Percy, 2nd Earl of Northumberland (1394–1455)

One of the great northern magnates, Henry Percy's long experience from the Scottish Borders seems to have been no preparation for urban fighting in the south of England. At St Albans in 1455 he was not given a specific command defending any of the Bars, but instead seems to have formed part of the king's bodyguard, and was killed near him.

in a letter: 'Here you saw one fall with his brains dashed out, there another with a broken arm, a third with a cut throat, and a fourth with a pierced chest, and the whole street was full of dead corpses.'

Those of the Lancastrians who were not killed or wounded fled in panic, in many cases throwing away their weapons and armour to aid their flight. The injured King Henry was helped to a humble refuge, a tanner's cottage, to have his wound treated, crying plaintively, 'Forsooth, forsooth! You do foully to smite a King annointed so!' Accounts differ as to whether he was wounded in the neck or the shoulder. The wound was probably only a minor scratch, but, to the medieval mind, for the blood of an anointed king to be shed in this way was shocking. When York heard that the king had been discovered, he ordered that Henry be escorted to the Abbey for safety until the fighting was finished. York must have been relieved to hear that the king was safe and in Yorkist hands, but he still needed to deal with Somerset and ensure that the duke did not escape from the town in the confusion of the battle. In fact Somerset and some of his men had taken shelter in the Castle Inn, one of the buildings just off the market place. They were quickly surrounded by the victorious Yorkists and, with no means of escape possible, Somerset rushed out of the building to die fighting, surrounded by his enemies. According to the Dijon Relation:

> York's men at once began to fight Somerset and his men, who were within the house and defended themselves valiantly. In the end, after the doors were broken down, Somerset saw he

had no option but to come out with his men, as a result of which they were all surrounded by the Duke of York's men. After some were stricken down and the Duke of Somerset had killed four men with his own hand, so it is said, he was felled to the ground with an axe, and at once wounded in so many places that he died.

In later years a legend was told that it had been prophesied that Somerset would die in the shadow of a castle. As a result he had always shunned visiting castles, but when he found himself trapped in the Castle Inn he realized he was doomed. The legend was so popular that it was mentioned by Shakespeare. In *Henry VI Part 2* (Act 5, Scene II), when York gazes on the dead Duke of Somerset he says:

So, lie thou there,
For underneath an alehouse' paltry sign
The 'Castle' in St Albans, Somerset
Hath made the wizard famous in his death.

'The wizard' was a reference to Roger Bolingbroke from Act 1 Scene IV.

Skipton Building Society, site of the Castle Inn. *Mike Elliott*

ON THIS SITE STOOD
THE CASTLE INN
BEFORE WHICH
EDMUND BEAUFORT
2ND DUKE OF SOMERSET,
WAS SLAIN DURING
THE 1ST BATTLE OF ST ALBANS
22ND MAY 1455.

As well as those who had been killed, many of the noblemen around King Henry had been badly wounded in the storm of Yorkist arrows. Buckingham was wounded in the face and neck and was taken to the Abbey for shelter. Buckingham's heir, Humphrey, Earl of Stafford was wounded in the hand. Somerset's heir, the nineteen-year-old Henry Beaufort, Earl of Dorset, described by a contemporary as 'a handsome young knight', was also wounded and had to be taken away in a cart – to one of Warwick's holdings, there to recuperate in his custody, thus adding insult to injury. John Sutton, 1st Baron Dudley, and John Wenlock, later 1st Baron Wenlock, a former Speaker of the House of Commons, were two more noblemen recorded as being wounded by arrows (Wenlock being the only such Yorkist casualty recorded).

Wenlock was taken in a cart all the way back to Dunstable. He would go on to have a colourful, if somewhat dubious, career during the Wars of the Roses. Wounded fighting for the Lancastrians at St Albans, he later changed sides and served the Yorkists, only eventually to change sides yet again and rejoin the Lancastrians. He was killed at the Battle of Tewkesbury in 1471, fighting for the Lancastrians but killed by his own side (allegedly by Somerset's grandson) when he was suspected of treachery.

The few noblemen who were not killed or wounded had their armour and horses stolen and their goods plundered. As Benet stated in his account of the battle, 'All who were on the side of Somerset were killed, wounded, or, at the least despoiled.'

It could have been worse. Later in the wars both sides became more ruthless, and enemy noblemen captured in battle were promptly executed by the victors. On this occasion the Yorkists were satisfied to have disposed of Somerset and regained control of the king. Most of the prisoners were soon released.

York now made his way to the Abbey and sent a message to the king, demanding that Buckingham and James Butler, Earl of Wiltshire be surrendered to the Yorkists. The king was warned that if these two noblemen were not immediately handed over, York and his men would enter the Abbey and take them by force.

Arrowheads. The broader, barbed heads are for use against animals, while the long pointed armour-piercing 'bodkins' are for military use, and devastated Henry VI's bodyguard and household. *Mike Elliott*

The king was left with little choice and the injured Buckingham was duly surrendered. Wiltshire, however, could not be found and it was rumoured that, abandoning his fine clothes and other possessions, he had fled the town disguised in a monk's habit. Wiltshire's conduct was widely criticized. Benet describes him as fleeing in panic from the battle (as he would do again after Mortimer's Cross in 1461). Gregory's Chronicle states that he was given the responsibility of carrying the Royal Standard but left it propped against the end of a house. According to Gregory, Wiltshire was reluctant to fight, as he was 'fearful of losing his beauty, for he was named the fairest knight of this land'. However, we need to treat this story with some caution, for, as we have seen, both Sir Philip Wentworth and Lord Sudeley were named as being responsible for carrying the Royal Standard. Wiltshire's luck finally ran out in March 1461 when he was captured and executed after the Battle of Towton.

One of the most persistent myths associated with the battle is the story that Queen Margaret of Anjou was present in St Albans to witness the Lancastrian defeat and that she had also taken shelter in the Abbey. This idea appears to have originated with Shakespeare, who was often willing to distort historic facts if he

Someries Castle, Sir John Wenlock's country seat (now almost on the runway at Luton Airport). *Mike Elliott*

thought that he could add to the theatrical drama. For Shakespeare, Margaret has to personally witness Somerset being cut down to incite her to commit the subsequent murders of Salisbury and Rutland after Wakefield in 1460. In fact, all the evidence suggests that Margaret and the Prince of Wales were in Greenwich at the time of the battle.

Once Buckingham had been handed over, York, Salisbury and Warwick entered the Abbey and approached the king. On bended knees they begged his forgiveness for having put his life in peril. They assured the king that they were loyal subjects who never meant to harm him, only the traitors around him such as Somerset. Henry forgave them – he obviously had little choice in the matter – and any threats to have them hanged, drawn and quartered were conveniently forgotten. King Henry 'took them to grace and so desired them to cease their people and that there should no more harm be done'.

As the king was clearly aware, it had become a matter of urgency to bring the Yorkist army under control. Although all organized resistance had ceased some time before with the death of Somerset, Yorkist soldiers were still rampaging through the town, looting and pillaging Lancastrians and townsfolk alike. Even a wealthy and important churchman like William Percy, Bishop of Carlisle, was not safe. Stripped of his horses, jewels and fine clothes, the bishop had to flee from the town on foot. Probably

York, Salisbury and Warwick thought that allowing the looting to continue was an easy and cheap way of rewarding their followers, but now York ordered an immediate cessation of the fighting in the king's name, and the mayhem was gradually brought under control.

Thus ended the First Battle of St Albans. The reasons for the overwhelming Yorkist victory are not difficult to find. Clearly the Duke of York had learned a great deal from his abortive rebellion three years before. This time the Yorkists had acted with speed, boldness and resolution. By secretly assembling a small but well-equipped and experienced army, they had gained a strategic advantage over the Lancastrians and they managed to stay one step ahead of them throughout the short campaign. By contrast, the men around King Henry had been hesitant and uncertain how to deal with the Yorkist challenge. They never managed to assemble an adequate military force to deal with the situation; instead they had unsuccessfully tried to achieve a peaceful political settlement. Ultimately, Buckingham's conviction that a peaceful compromise could still be reached with the Yorkists proved disastrous.

While the main course of events during the battle is not in dispute, there is considerable uncertainty over the actual timing of these events. When did the battle start? How much time elapsed between the initial attacks and Warwick's breakthrough into the town? And finally, how long did the battle last? The problem is complicated by the fact that there seem to have been two types of time-keeping in the medieval period. The first was by the twenty-four-hour clock (as used by the church and perhaps ecclesiastical chroniclers), and the second was by counting the hours from sunrise.

The Dijon Relation states that the battle started at exactly 10 a.m., but other accounts suggest that it may have started later, possibly some time between 11 a.m. and twelve noon. The Dijon Relation also states that the battle went on for some hours, finishing at 2.30 p.m., while the Paston letters state that the battle was fought and won in little more than half an hour. In trying to reconcile these different accounts, some writers have suggested that the fighting at the barriers went on for an hour before Warwick launched his attack, but considering the relatively small casualty list, and the fact that many of the Lancastrian noblemen had not completed putting on their full suits of armour, this does not seem very likely. It is probable that the main part of the fighting was indeed over in half an hour; however, the looting, pillaging and sacking of St Albans appears to have continued for some hours after organized resistance had ceased.

In purely military terms, the First Battle of St Albans was a small-scale affair, more like an ugly street brawl or a skirmish than a full-scale battle. Total casualties from the battle were remarkably light. The Dijon Relation states that 200 men were killed, the Paston letters have a figure of 120 killed, and Benet writes of 100 killed. The best modern estimates are that the total number of those killed lay between 60 and 120. This is a remarkably small number, and far fewer than in any other major battle during the Wars of the Roses. However, a disproportionate number of the casualties were of noble blood. As well as Somerset, Northumberland and Clifford, there were many knights, squires and members of the king's personal household killed. The fact that the only three Lancastrian peers to be killed just happened to be the three men that the Yorkists most wanted to be rid of is highly suspicious, and suggests that York and the Nevilles had no intention of ever taking them prisoner.

Some later Tudor historians, writing long after the event, exaggerated the casualty figures and wrote of many hundreds or even thousands being killed. There is no evidence to suggest that such figures are accurate, and they may well derive from confusion with the casualty figures from the Second Battle of St Albans. The members of the king's household who were killed in the battle were buried in the Abbey, and some of the Lancastrian nobles – particularly Northumberland, Somerset and Lord Clifford – were also buried below the floor of the Lady Chapel, where the memory of these three tombs long outlived their destruction in the Reformation.

The Lady Chapel, St Albans Abbey. Somerset, Northumberland and Clifford were buried here after the first battle. *By kind permission of St Albans Abbey. Photograph: John Kliene*

Although the battle was a minor affair from a military point of view, its political effects were profound. It proved to be just the first round in the Wars of the Roses, a conflict that raged on for the next thirty-two years, the longest period of civil strife in English history. In one respect the battle was the culmination of the long-running feud between York and Somerset. However, the battle had not simply been between the two dukes – it had also involved King Henry, and this gave it a much greater significance. Although Henry was a weak and ineffectual individual, he was still the king, and as such he represented the supreme political authority in the realm. The events of the battle, with Henry being wounded and taken prisoner, members of his household being slaughtered around him, and the Royal Standard trampled in the dust, brutally revealed a fundamental weakness at the heart of the monarchy. After the battle the Yorkists treated Henry with all due respect, but this could not disguise the fact that a line had been crossed and the prestige of the monarchy would not be easily restored.

While on the one hand the battle had brutally demonstrated the weakness of the monarchy under Henry VI, it had at the same time brought fame and glory to the Earl of Warwick, and launched him on the career that would make him one of the most important figures in English politics for the next seventeen years, eventually earning him the nickname of 'Warwick the Kingmaker'. As Paul Murray Kendall states in his biography of Warwick:

> But the Earl of Warwick's position had altered. To the fifteenth century, war was still the birthplace of glory. Though Sir Robert Ogle led the decisive assault at St Albans, he was a captain in Warwick's command, and the emblems of the Ragged Staff had shone brightly in St Peter's Street. Warwick's dashing attack had won him a military reputation and a sudden fame.

On Friday 23rd the Yorkists escorted the king back to London. The Duke of York rode on the king's right, the Earl of Salisbury on his left, and the Earl of Warwick rode in front carrying the Sword of State. Although the Yorkists treated Henry with the utmost respect, it was obvious to everyone that the balance of power had dramatically shifted and, for the moment at least, York and the Nevilles were the real power behind the throne.

Chapter 3

THE WAR RENEWED

TO UNDERSTAND WHY A second battle came to be fought in St Albans in 1461, and between some of the same people, we need to see how fortune's wheel had turned several times in the wars in the intervening six years.

Four years of uneasy peace had followed the First Battle and there was a desperate hope that after the bloodshed that had occurred any remaining political disputes could be resolved peacefully. For a while this hope helped to prevent any further outbreaks of large-scale conflict.

By their victory the Yorkists appeared to have achieved all that they had hoped for. The Duke of Somerset had been disposed of and the Duke of York now assumed the role of Constable of England, while the Earl of Warwick was made Captain of Calais. This latter post was of great importance. During the Wars of the Roses whoever controlled Calais not only had a well-fortified harbour directly opposite the coast of Kent, they also commanded the Calais garrison, which included almost 1,000 professional soldiers, a significant military force at a time when England lacked a regular standing army.

For the Lancastrians, St Albans had been a major disaster, and Margaret of Anjou was more convinced than ever that the power of the Yorkist faction had to be destroyed if her young son was ever to succeed to the throne. Margaret could count on powerful support from the families of the noblemen killed at St Albans, these being the Earl of Northumberland, Lord Clifford and the Duke of Somerset. The slain Somerset was succeeded by his son, Henry Beaufort, who became the 3rd Duke of Somerset. The fallen Earl of Northumberland and Lord Clifford were also succeeded by their sons. Thus the Lancastrian cause was taken over by a younger generation of men to whom the wars were not just a political dispute but also a personal feud. In particular, John, 9th Lord Clifford was determined to exact revenge for his father's death.

Margaret ensured that Lancastrian supporters gradually replaced Yorkist supporters in most of the key offices of state. Her plans to replace Warwick with the young Somerset as Captain of Calais came to nought, but she continued her intrigues to have Warwick removed from this key post. Margaret began organizing support for the Lancastrians in the Midlands, and from September

1456 onwards she and the king tended to avoid pro-Yorkist London and spent more and more time in Coventry, which became the *de facto* capital.

In August 1457 tension was increased when French raiders landed in Kent and proceeded to sack and pillage the coastal town of Sandwich. There was a widespread fear that the attack on Sandwich might be the prelude to a full-scale French invasion, and it seemed more imperative than ever to avoid a further outbreak of civil war. Attempts to preserve the peace reached a climax in early 1458, when King Henry commanded a great Council to assemble in London, to settle 'such variances as be betwixt divers Lords of our Realm'.

However, the fear and suspicion that existed was soon evident to everyone, for as the great lords arrived they were accompanied by large well-armed retinues, which amounted to a series of private armies. The Mayor of London had to make great efforts to keep the two sides apart and preserve law and order.

Despite all the tensions the Council managed to make some progress towards agreement. York, Salisbury and Warwick promised to found a perpetual Chantry at St Albans to sing masses for the souls of all those slain in the battle. York also agreed to pay 5,000 marks in compensation to the widowed Duchess of Somerset, and Warwick was to pay 1,000 marks to the Clifford family. At the end of the Council on what came to be called the 'Love-day', 24 March 1458, the king went in solemn state to St Paul's Cathedral for a ceremony of peace and reconciliation. He was preceded by the principal antagonists marching two by two: the Earl of Salisbury with the young Duke of Somerset, the Earl of Warwick with the Earl of Northumberland, and even the Duke of York walking alongside Queen Margaret. To the spectators who were there to witness this improbable scene, it seemed that all the tensions and turbulence of the previous years were finally resolved. However, England's problems proved to be too great and too complex to be solved by empty theatrical gestures such as the 'Love-day'. During the next fourteen years almost every one of the principal players at this scene would meet a violent death – either killed in battle, executed, or murdered.

During the summer of 1458 Warwick assembled a squadron of ships at Calais and used them to suppress the French and Burgundian pirates. He also led his men on privateering raids on the Spanish and Hanseatic merchant fleets. This helped to enhance his reputation as a bold and daring commander, with the added bonus of enabling him to continue paying the garrison at Calais. The English had been starved of military victories for the previous thirty years and most people were thrilled by news of

Warwick's exploits. However, foreign ambassadors were less impressed and they accused Warwick and his men of piracy. Margaret utilized these accusations to demand that Warwick should come to London and explain his actions, but when he eventually arrived at the Palace of Westminster in October the meeting turned into a fiasco. The queen and Warwick's servants started fighting each other and when Warwick tried to intervene he was almost stabbed. Warwick fled from the scene convinced that he had been the victim of an attempted assassination and that the queen could not be trusted.

By the summer of 1459 the country was once more drifting into full-scale civil war. Margaret had continued to gather support throughout the Midlands and in June she and King Henry decided that they were strong enough to call a Great Council at Coventry. York, Warwick and Salisbury were deliberately not invited; instead the Council accused them of treason. To defend themselves, the Yorkist leadership decided to gather their forces and meet at Ludlow. Warwick brought with him some 600 well-trained men from the Calais garrison. One of their commanders, Andrew Trollope, was a well-known professional soldier. However, the loyalty of these men was suspect. Warwick was a popular commander, but his men were still strongly influenced by their oath of allegiance to the king. As a result Warwick felt obliged to promise his men that they would not be expected to fight against the king.

Serious fighting broke out before the Yorkists even reached Ludlow. On 23 September 1459 Salisbury was intercepted at Blore Heath near Market Drayton by a Lancastrian force commanded by Lord Audley, who had been given orders by the queen to arrest Salisbury. The resulting battle was the first major clash between the Yorkists and Lancastrians since St Albans. It resulted in a dramatic Yorkist victory and Audley himself was killed in the fighting, but the Yorkist victory did little to alter the overall strategic situation. Salisbury knew that King Henry and Queen Margaret were approaching with a large army and that same night he slipped away, anxious to join forces with York and Warwick before his outnumbered army was overwhelmed.

The Yorkists united their forces at Ludlow, where they planned to take up a strongly fortified position on the banks of the River Teme, but it soon became obvious that they were heavily outnumbered, and furthermore the loyalty of some of their men could not be relied on. On 13 October the Lancastrian Army approached the Yorkists' position and announced that the king was offering a pardon to anyone who deserted the Yorkist cause and joined him. This resulted in Trollope and a large number of men from Calais defecting *en masse*. The Yorkist leadership now realized that the position was hopeless, and abandoning their army they slipped away that night. The triumphant Lancastrians celebrated their success by brutally sacking and plundering Ludlow.

York, together with his second son, Edmund, Earl of Rutland, fled to Ireland, and Salisbury, Warwick and York's eldest son, Edward, Earl of March fled to Calais. In the aftermath of the fiasco at Ludlow it seemed that the Yorkist victories at St Albans and Blore Heath had achieved nothing. The Yorkist cause was in ruins and Margaret and the Lancastrians effectively ruled the country. In November 1459 Margaret had Parliament meet in Coventry. Parliament obligingly condemned twenty-seven leading Yorkists as traitors. Their estates were to be confiscated and their heirs disinherited.

Events soon began to show, however, that the Lancastrians were not as secure as at first appeared. York was popular in Ireland and was soon in effective control of the whole country. Meanwhile the rest of the Yorkists were safe behind the walls of Calais. Somerset was appointed Captain of Calais and despatched with a small army to seize control of the town. He was assisted by the redoubtable Trollope, who had personal knowledge of the Calais defences. Somerset made little progress and it soon became clear that he urgently needed reinforcements. A force was assembled at Sandwich under the command of Richard Woodville, Lord Rivers, but on 15 January 1460 a raiding force from Calais attacked Sandwich, scattered the Lancastrian force and captured Lord Rivers while he was still in bed. Sandwich thus had the unusual distinction of having been raided by both the French and the English within a few years of each other. To complete their victory, the jubilant Yorkists then seized the ships in the harbour, which had been gathered to transport the reinforcements, and sailed them back in triumph to Calais.

By June 1460 the Yorkists had decided that the time had come to go on the offensive. Salisbury, Warwick and March landed at Sandwich with a force of some 2,000 men. The customary manifestos were issued, announcing that the Yorkists were loyal to the king, but his evil advisers had to be removed or else they would bring ruin to the country. Thousands of new recruits flocked to join the Yorkist cause and were able to march through Kent virtually unopposed. On 2 July the Yorkists entered London.

As soon as King Henry learned of the Yorkist landing in Kent, he bade farewell to his wife and son and, leaving Coventry, marched south with his army to meet this new threat. By the time the Lancastrians had reached Northampton they had learned that the Yorkists had managed to raise a large army and occupy London.

Henry and the Lancastrian lords decided to wait at Northampton for reinforcements before they advanced any further. They occupied a strong position just south of the town in a bend of the River Nene. The river protected the Lancastrians' rear and flanks. They protected their front by digging a ditch and earthworks. The ditch was then flooded with water from the Nene, and cannon were placed behind the earthworks to cover their front. Meanwhile Warwick and March had left London and were marching north with the bulk of the Yorkist army, leaving Salisbury behind to hold the city.

The Battle of Northampton was fought on 10 July 1460 but turned into a disaster for the Lancastrians. Heavy rain had flooded their entrenchments and made their gunpowder damp, resulting in most of their cannons being unable to fire. Then Lord Grey of Ruthyn, commanding the Lancastrian right wing, betrayed the cause. When the Yorkist left wing attacked Grey's men they put up no resistance and actually assisted the Yorkists to cross the ditch and earthworks. By the end of the battle King Henry was a prisoner and many leading Lancastrians were killed. Many of the Lancastrian casualties were apparently drowned as, panic-stricken, they tried to flee across the river.

After the battle the victorious Yorkists escorted King Henry back to London in scenes that must have been strangely reminiscent of the events after the First Battle of St Albans. Warwick was able to sail back to Calais to deal with the threat from Somerset. The Yorkist victory at Northampton had completely changed the situation and Somerset agreed to disband his army before going into exile in France. Meanwhile the Yorkist leadership waited for York to join them from Ireland. York finally landed at Chester in September and slowly made his way across the country, accompanied by a splendid retinue of soldiers and servants. Disturbing rumours soon reached London that York was considering seizing the throne and declaring himself king. He was reported to be displaying banners emblazoned with the Royal Arms of England and to have his sword carried upright before him as if it was the Sword of State. York finally arrived in London on 10 October and went straight to the Palace of Westminster. In front of the assembled peers he walked up to the empty throne and placed his hand on it. It was a dramatic moment: any new King of England was expected to receive the acclamation of the peers before seating himself on the throne. Nobody present could have mistaken the meaning of York's gesture, but when York turned eagerly to the peers expecting their acclamation there was instead a dismayed silence. York had seriously overplayed his hand. Most of the assembled peers were well aware that the feeble-minded

Henry was unfit to be king. They also probably detested Margaret and her advisers, and were hoping that York and Warwick could provide the country with firm government, but they still felt themselves bound by their oath of allegiance to King Henry.

York stood by the empty throne, growing increasingly angry, until eventually the Archbishop of Canterbury intervened, going up to the duke and asking if York would go with him to see the king. York angrily replied: 'I do not recall that I know anyone in the kingdom whom it would not befit to come to me, and see me rather than I should go and visit him.'

Eventually a compromise was reached. On 24 October 1460 Parliament passed an Act of Accord. Henry was to retain the title of King of England for the rest of his life, but York and his heirs were recognized as the rightful heirs to the throne. Margaret's son was declared to be illegitimate, and to have no claim to the throne. The Act of Accord guaranteed future conflict, for Margaret would never accept a settlement that excluded her son from the throne.

When Margaret heard the news of Northampton she had fled to Wales with her young son and just a handful of servants. Some of the servants proved untrustworthy – Margaret had her money and jewellery stolen, and lived in constant fear of being kidnapped and handed over to the Yorkists. It was only after a series of perilous adventures that Margaret reached the safety of Harlech Castle. Eventually Margaret ordered her supporter, Jasper Tudor, Earl of Pembroke, to organize resistance in Wales, before taking ship to Scotland where she hoped to gather further support. Meanwhile the Lancastrian peers were recovering from the shock of Northampton and gathering a large army in Yorkshire. Northumberland probably took the lead but he was soon joined by the stalwarts of the Lancastrian cause, Lords Clifford and Roos, Sir Thomas Courtenay, Earl of Devon, James Butler, Earl of Wiltshire and Henry Holland, Earl of Exeter. They were also joined by Somerset, who returned from exile in France together with Trollope. Ominous rumours were soon reaching London that the Lancastrians had gathered an army of 15,000 to 20,000 men in Yorkshire. It was obvious that the Yorkists had missed a golden opportunity to end the war after Northampton; instead of marching north and crushing all opposition, they had allowed themselves to become distracted by their attempts to reach a political settlement.

Action needed to be taken urgently and it was decided that Warwick would hold London and keep control of the king. York's eldest son, nineteen-year-old Edward, Earl of March would have his first independent command, leading a small army to keep an eye on Pembroke and the Lancastrian supporters in Wales.

Meanwhile York, Salisbury and York's second son, the Earl of Rutland, would march north to deal with the main Lancastrian force in Yorkshire.

York left London on 9 December with an army of some 8,000 men and reached Sandal Castle, just south of Wakefield, on 21 December, where he spent a miserable Christmas, short of provisions, and facing a much larger Lancastrian army.

Nonetheless, York should have been secure had he stayed in Sandal Castle and awaited reinforcements. However, on 30 December he sallied out of the castle and found himself facing a much stronger Lancastrian force. It is hard to understand why an experienced commander like York made such a foolish mistake. Various suggestions have been made but the most likely explanation is that the Lancastrians tricked York out of Sandal Castle by attacking one of his foraging parties, in sight of the castle, with a small force, while the rest of their force remained hidden in the woods. Once York had committed himself the main force emerged to cut off his retreat and York was trapped, 'like a fish in a net, or a deer in a buckstall'.

Salisbury and the remaining men in the castle came out to assist, but it was too little and too late to affect the outcome. Surrounded and outnumbered, the Yorkists were slaughtered, over 2,000 being killed. York himself died bravely, fighting sword in hand until he was overwhelmed.

Rutland and his tutor Sir Robert Aspall tried to flee but were recognized in Wakefield by Clifford, who killed them both. It was this incident that earned Clifford the nickname 'Bloody Clifford' or 'Black-faced Clifford'. Later writers greatly embroidered this incident: Rutland was portrayed as a young child, kneeling and pleading for his life, but we need to treat these stories with a great deal of caution. In fact Rutland was seventeen at the time of Wakefield. In medieval society he would have been regarded as an adult, expected to carry weapons, wear armour, and play an active part in the battle. This of course does not excuse Clifford's actions, but it is probably an exaggeration to describe him as a child-killer.

A different fate awaited Salisbury: he was captured alive and taken to Pontefract Castle. He agreed to pay a large ransom in exchange for being released, but the same night a Lancastrian mob stormed into the castle, dragged him outside and beheaded him. It is possible that Northumberland, determined to avenge his father's death at St Albans, was involved in this affair. Wakefield was a good opportunity for the Lancastrians to settle old scores!

The severed heads of York, Rutland and Salisbury were impaled on the spikes of the Micklegate Bar in the city of York. Lancastrians joked that 'York could look upon York', and a paper

Bisham Abbey, the Nevilles' southern base, where Salisbury was buried after Wakefield and then Warwick and Montagu after Barnet. *John Hurst*

crown was placed on York's head mocking his ambition to become king. It was said that two spikes were deliberately left empty so that they could eventually be adorned with the heads of March and Warwick.

A jubilant Queen Margaret travelled down from Scotland to greet the victorious Lancastrian army. At York, the Lancastrian peers solemnly renewed their oath of fealty to the queen and acknowledged her son as rightful heir to the throne. The Lancastrians were now faced with a choice. They could consolidate their position in the north of England and build up their army for a spring campaign, but this would risk losing the offer of immediate Scottish support. Alternatively, they could exploit the momentum created by their victory and immediately march on London, gambling on speed and nerve and aiming to give the Yorkists little time to raise a fresh army. They chose the latter course and this dictated the whole nature of their 1461 winter campaign. Impressing untrained men as they went, and living off the land, the army left York on 20 January, and started their march on London.

Chapter 4

1461: THE WINTER CAMPAIGN

AT THE BEGINNING OF 1461 a wave of terror swept across southern England. The Battle of Wakefield had been a disastrous defeat for the Yorkists, with the Duke of York and the Earls of Salisbury and Rutland being killed. Flushed with victory, Queen Margaret and the young Edward, Prince of Wales, were now leading a huge army south, and the Lancastrian advance was accompanied by widespread burning, looting, raping and pillaging. With Margaret rode a glittering array of the leading Lancastrian peers: the Duke of Somerset, the Duke of Exeter, the Earl of Northumberland, the Earl of Devon, the Earl of Shrews-bury, Lord Clifford, Lord Roos, Lord Grey of Codnor, Lord Fitzhugh, Lord Greystoke, Lord Welles and Lord Welles and Willoughby (father and son). All these noblemen wore the prince's badge of a bend of black and red with ostrich feathers, thus demonstrating their loyalty to the prince and their rejection of the Act of Accord which had made the House of York heirs to the throne.

As well as the Lancastrian peers and their supporters, Margaret's army included French, Scottish and Welsh mer-cenaries. Margaret had been in Scotland when the Battle of Wakefield had been fought. Throughout the Middle Ages the kings of Scotland had always been willing to take advantage when England was distracted by problems, be it foreign wars abroad or civil war at home. The Wars of the Roses were no exception. The previous year, 1460, King James II of Scotland had led an army against Roxburgh Castle. The castle had eventually been captured, but not before James himself had been killed when one of the Scottish cannons had accidentally exploded. The new King, James III, was only nine years old and real power was in the hands of his mother, Mary of Guelders. Mary agreed to supply Queen Margaret with Scottish soldiers; in return the young Prince Edward would be betrothed to James III's equally young sister, Margaret Stewart, and the long-disputed town and castle of Berwick would be handed over to the Scots. It was an excellent bargain for Mary of Guelders, with the added bonus of despatching some of Mary's more turbulent subjects to cause trouble in England instead of making a nuisance of themselves at home. Most Englishmen, however, were outraged over the surrender of Berwick. This deal was all too typical of Queen

Ermine Street at Hertford Heath before metalling, showing the Roman layout. Watling Street, later on the same march, would have looked very much the same. *R. Lydekker,* Cambridge County Geographies: Hertfordshire, *Cambridge University Press, 1909*

Margaret, pursuing short-term dynastic gains while ignoring England's long-term interests and playing into the hands of Yorkist propaganda.

The Lancastrians had also been recruiting from both sides of the Anglo-Scottish border. In the late Middle Ages this border region was a notoriously violent and lawless area, which neither the kings of England nor Scotland were able to control effectively. On both sides of the border lived the border reivers, hard-riding, hard-fighting bands of men to whom cross-border raids and cattle stealing were a way of life. Many of these men would have had little interest in the Lancastrian cause, but the opportunity to plunder and pillage the prosperous lands of southern England brought them flocking to Margaret's banners. The mercenaries and volunteers, though, still did not provide enough men for the assault on the south, and the Lancastrians impressed unwilling Yorkshiremen into the army with the promise of loot for them too.

As the Lancastrian army slowly advanced down the old Roman road of Ermine Street, it left a thirty-mile-wide swathe of destruction in its wake. The towns of Grantham, Stamford, Peterborough, Huntingdon and Royston suffered particularly severely, and a wave of horror swept across southern England as reports of Margaret's progress spread. Contemporary accounts all agree about the scale of the destruction. According to the Chronicle of the Abbey of Croyland,

> The duke [of York] being thus removed from this world, the north men, being sensible that the only impediment was now withdrawn, and that there was no one now who would care to resist their inroads, again swept onwards like a whirlwind from the north, and in the impulse of their fury attempted to overrun the whole of England. At this period too, fancying

that every thing tended to insure them freedom from molestation, paupers and beggars flocked forth from those quarters in infinite numbers, just like so many mice rushing forth from their holes, and universally devoted themselves to spoil and rapine, without regard of place or person ...

Thus did they proceed with impunity, spreading in vast multitudes over a space of thirty miles in breadth, and, covering the whole surface of the earth just like so many locusts, made their way to the very walls of London.

Davies' English Chronicle was equally horrified by the behaviour of the Lancastrian army, 'robbing all the country and the people as they came, spoiling Abbeys, houses of religion and churches, and bearing away chalices, books and other ornaments, as if they had been pagans or Saracens and not Christian men'.

Abbot John Whethamstede had previously been sympathetic to the Lancastrian cause, but it is clear from his account that he was also outraged by the looting and pillaging of Margaret's army:

[The northern men] with the Queen and Prince took their way towards the southern parts, and advanced without interruption by a good route until they came to the town and monastery of the English protomartyr Alban; and in every place through which they came on both sides of the Trent, but especially on this side, they robbed, despoiled and devastated, and carried off with them whatever they could come upon or discover, whether garments or money, herds of cattle or single animals, or any other thing whatsoever, sparing neither churches nor clergy, monasteries nor monks, chapels nor chaplains.

Was Margaret unable to control her undisciplined army, or had she, as the Yorkists claimed, promised her followers that they could loot and pillage as a cheap way of paying them? Whatever the truth, it proved to be a major strategic blunder. The behaviour of Margaret's army rallied support to the Yorkist cause across southern England. Ironically, Margaret's more undisciplined and less willing followers proved to be of little military value; happy to loot and pillage, they deserted wholesale when faced by the prospect of a full-scale battle at St Albans.

The deaths of York and Salisbury at Wakefield meant that the leadership of the Yorkist cause was now in the hands of a younger generation, York's eldest son the Earl of March and Salisbury's eldest son the Earl of Warwick. As soon as word reached London of the disaster at Wakefield, Warwick and his allies started to gather their forces in order to oppose the Lancastrian advance. The London Council loaned Warwick 2,000 marks 'for the defence of the Realm'. Warwick issued several Commissions of Array, the Duke of Norfolk was sent to East Anglia to raise men, and at the same time the Earl of Arundel, Viscount Bourchier and Lord Bonville were sent to raise men in the southern counties. Other Yorkist peers were told to call up their retainers. As news of the Lancastrian advance spread, many men did not even wait to be summoned but made their way to London, ready to join Warwick's army. Meanwhile, castles were garrisoned, curfews were imposed and Warwick's brother, George Neville, the Chancellor sent out a stream of writs. Orders were despatched for the maintenance of order, the arrest of rebels and rioters, those holding unlawful assemblies, those uttering false tidings and anyone trying to hinder the lawful defence of the king. Orders were sent to the ports of Norfolk telling them not to permit the shipment of provisions to the Lancastrian army. The Council continued to be concerned about events in Norfolk, and on 7 February it ordered the seizure of Castle Rising, when it was reported that the owner, Thomas Daniel, was plotting a Lancastrian uprising in the county. The castle was seized, but Daniel himself escaped and rode north to join Margaret's army.

The international sphere was not neglected either. Warwick sent letters to the Duke of Milan, the Pope and Philip of Burgundy, expressing confidence in the future and trying to minimize the significance of the defeat at Wakefield. The Duke of Burgundy sent a contingent of Burgundian mercenaries to Warwick, but most foreign rulers were cautious about taking sides and preferred to wait on events.

Despite all this frantic activity, Warwick was reluctant to issue the crucial orders to march his army into the Midlands and intercept Margaret's northern hordes. Instead, he busied himself with issues which had little to do with the immediate military crisis: for example, he ensured that he inherited his father's largely symbolic office of Great Chamberlain of England, he raised his brother, John Neville, to the peerage with the title of Lord Montagu, and on 8 February he had himself, Sir John Wenlock, Lord Bonville and Sir Thomas Kyriell elected to the Order of the Garter with great pomp and ceremony. Warwick had established his reputation at St Albans, at Northampton, and as the Captain of Calais by his willingness to seize the initiative, his bold and daring attacks, but now it seemed that his confidence had deserted him and he was reluctant to face battle without the support of his ally, the Earl of March.

March had earlier been given his first independent command and despatched to the Welsh border. His task was to raise an army in the Marches and be in a position to deal with a possible Lancastrian uprising in Wales. One of the main Lancastrian supporters in the area was Owen Tudor, a Welsh nobleman and one-time courtier, who had married Henry V's widow Katherine of Valois, and fathered two sons. Owen Tudor was thus King Henry VI's stepfather, and his two sons were the king's half-brothers.

March was at Shrewsbury when he heard the dreadful news of the disaster at Wakefield. He immediately assembled his army and planned to march on London to reinforce Warwick. March was a determined young man and no doubt he was burning to avenge the deaths of his father and brother. However, before he could even start his march fresh tidings alerted him to a new danger. James Butler, Earl of Wiltshire had landed in south-west Wales with a force of Irish, French and Breton mercenaries. Wiltshire had then joined forces with one of Owen Tudor's sons, Jasper Tudor, Earl of Pembroke. The two earls were marching across Wales, raising new recruits and planning to join Queen Margaret's army. March decided that he must deal with this new threat first, and swiftly marched his army to intercept Wiltshire and Pembroke at the little village of Mortimer's Cross, near Wigmore Castle in Hereford-shire. Few details of the subsequent battle have survived and we cannot even be sure if the battle was fought on 2 or 3 February. We are told that on the morning of the battle March's men were shocked to see three suns in the sky. This unusual phenomenon is known as a Panhelion, and is caused by light shining through ice crystals in the atmosphere, but it is easy to imagine the feelings of fear and superstitious dread that uneducated medieval soldiers would have experienced at such an unusual sight. March rose to the occasion – he told his men that the three suns represented the Holy Trinity of the Father, the Son and the Holy Ghost. It meant that God was on their side and was promising them that victory would be theirs. March fell to his knees and gave thanks to God, before getting up and leading his men into battle. March never forgot this moment and he later adopted 'the Sun in Splendour' as his personal badge.

It seems likely that the Lancastrian army, containing as it did Welsh, Irish, English, French and Bretons, was not a very cohesive force, nor can they have had much confidence in their leaders. Wiltshire was best known for having fled from the First Battle of St Albans disguised as a monk. It is also probable that many of the Breton and Irish mercenaries were poorly armed and had little protection from the English archers. Certainly, the battle ended in a complete rout of the Lancastrian army. Wiltshire and Pembroke managed to escape, but Owen Tudor, and many other leading Lancastrians were taken prisoner. Edward, remembering the fate of the Yorkist prisoners after Wakefield, ordered that Tudor and eight of the other Lancastrian commanders be taken to Hereford and executed. It is said that Tudor, a popular and respected nobleman, could not believe that the Yorkists would really execute him. Only when the collar of his red velvet doublet was ripped from his shoulders did he realize that he was about to die. Sadly he remarked, 'That head shall lie on the stock that was wont to lie on Queen Katherine's lap.' After the execution, Tudor's severed head was placed on the top step of the market cross. Apparently, a local madwoman washed the face, combed the hair and placed lighted candles all around it.

The Battle of Mortimer's Cross was the first of March's great victories. His triumphs on the battlefield would not only make him King of England, but would also earn him a reputation as one of England's last and greatest warrior kings. After the disaster at Wakefield, the victory at Mortimer's Cross was a timely triumph which helped rally support for the Yorkist cause. However, it would seem that the escape of Wiltshire and Pembroke persuaded March that there was still a potential threat from the Lancastrians in Wales. For two vital weeks, instead of marching to reinforce Warwick's army in London, March remained inactive on the Welsh border. The result was that when Warwick's army faced

Effigies of the Earl and Countess of Arundel in the Fitzalan Chapel, Arundel Castle. The countess was Warwick's sister. Arundel was one of the peers in the Yorkist army that left London on 12 February 1461. *By kind permission of His Grace The Duke of Norfolk, Arundel Castle.*

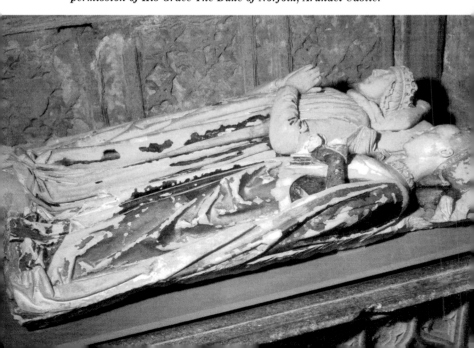

Margaret's northern hordes at St Albans, March's army was still far away to the west.

On the morning of 12 February Warwick finally left London and marched to St Albans. He was accompanied by King Henry, Norfolk, Suffolk, Arundel, his brother Lord Montagu, and Lords Berners, Bonville, Bourchier and Fauconberg. (We have listed Fauconberg here because some authorities do place him with Warwick in February 1461. Other authorities, however, place him elsewhere and there seems to be no definitive contemporary account of his full movements before his arrival at Towton. If he was at St Albans then he deserves special mention as the only active combatant at both battles to have changed sides between them.) It has been estimated that in total there were nine Yorkist peers, opposed to twelve Lancastrian peers in Queen Margaret's army. However, it should not be assumed that this ratio was necessarily reflected in the number of fighting men present on each side. The course of the campaign now began to resemble a curious mirror image of the events of 1455. Whereas in 1455 the Yorkists had been marching on London with a northern army, now in 1461 the Lancastrians were doing exactly the same. In 1455 the Lancastrians had been defending St Albans; in 1461 it was the Yorkists who were trying to hold the town. Warwick's decision to place his army at St Albans meant that for a second time in less than six years the town would become a bloody battlefield.

Chapter 5

THE SECOND BATTLE OF ST ALBANS

THE EARL OF WARWICK and the Yorkist army reached St Albans on the evening of 12 February. Warwick apparently did not intend to fight a battle within the town, but instead deployed most of his army to the north of St Albans. Warwick's army appears to have been divided into the three traditional divisions: the vanguard, or right wing, under the Duke of Norfolk potentially as far north as Nomansland Common; the centre, or main body, under Warwick in the village of Sandridge; and the rearguard, or left wing, under his younger brother, John Neville, the newly created Lord Montagu, just north of St Albans on Bernards Heath. There was also a strong detachment of archers in the centre of St Albans itself.

The Yorkists spent 13 to 16 February preparing elaborate defences to the north of St Albans. According to Gregory's Chronicle: 'The Lords in King Harry's party pitched a field and fortified it very strongly.'

They employed a number of devices which were normally used only in siege warfare. These included caltrops, iron nails twisted together so that no matter how they were dropped, one spike was always pointing upwards, and naval anti-boarding nets of thick cord, 24 feet long and 4 feet wide, set with spikes at the intersections. The caltrops would be scattered in large numbers in front of the Yorkist positions, and the nets would be strung across paths or gaps in hedges. They also used pavises, wooden boards that enabled archers and crossbowmen to shoot while remaining under cover themselves. The pavises sometimes had spikes in the front and could be dropped flat on the ground to provide an obstacle if an enemy came too close.

As well as these devices Warwick's Burgundian mercenaries were armed with cannons and a terrifying new weapon, the 'handgun'. These handguns, although crude and unreliable, were none the less the ancestors of the later muskets and rifles. The Second Battle of St Albans was probably the first time that such weapons had ever been used in battle on English soil.

According to Gregory, 'the Burgundians had such instruments that would shoot both pellets of lead and arrows of an ell in length with six feathers, three in the middle and three at one end, with a very big head of iron at the other end, and wild fire, all together.'

An ell is about 45 inches long, and it is highly unlikely that any

Handgun hooked over pavise, firing. *John Kliene*

kind of medieval handgun could have fired the kind of iron arrows that Gregory describes – presumably they were somehow fired from cannons. Gregory's reference to 'wild fire' probably refers to the use of petards, a type of crude bomb. They were filled with explosive combustibles and could be thrown at the enemy. Like the handgun, the petard often proved more lethal to the user than the opposition, hence the well-known expression: 'hoist with his own petard'.

As with many medieval battles, there is considerable uncertainty about the size of the armies involved. Estimates of Warwick's army range from 8,000 to 12,000 men. The size of the Lancastrian army is even harder to ascertain: Margaret probably had over 20,000 men with her when she left Yorkshire, but large-scale desertion had probably reduced this force to less than 15,000. The Second Battle of St Albans was obviously much larger than the first battle, with possibly five times as many men involved. Margaret theoretically had the advantage of numbers over Warwick, but her army was ill-disciplined and she had to rely on a relatively small hard core of professional soldiers.

When the Lancastrian army reached Royston, instead of continuing their advance on London, they swung west and marched

Icknield Way before metalling, the Stone Age trackway the Lancastrians used from Royston to Dunstable. *R. Lydekker*, Cambridge County Geographies: Hertfordshire, *Cambridge University Press, 1909*

the twenty-seven miles to Dunstable, reaching there on 16 February. We cannot be certain when the Lancastrians left Royston or the reasons for their sudden change of direction, but the probability is that they had received news of Warwick's presence at St Albans with King Henry and also of the defences that he was preparing to the north of the town. From Dunstable the Lancastrians could advance on St Albans down Watling Street. This would outflank Warwick's defences and enable them to attack the Yorkists from an unexpected direction. Dunstable was occupied by a small Yorkist force, apparently commanded by Sir Robert Poynings, one of Norfolk's retainers. Gregory, however, states that Dunstable was held by a force of several hundred men led by a local butcher, a man who knew nothing of warfare. It seems likely that the force Gregory refers to was made up of local townspeople who were encouraged by the presence of Poynings' men to arm themselves and to try and save the town from being sacked and pillaged. They could not have expected to find themselves facing the battle-hardened vanguard of the main Lancastrian army, and resistance was probably swiftly crushed. One of the main reasons for having an outpost at Dunstable was to warn Warwick of any Lancastrian advance from that direction, but there could have been few Yorkist survivors from the fight, for no word appears to have reached St Albans to which any credence was given. Gregory states that the local butcher was one of those who survived the fight but he afterwards hanged himself for shame and remorse at having led his men into a massacre.

The Lancastrian army did not halt at Dunstable but after a brief rest pushed on down Watling Street, marching through the night, towards St Albans, which lay just twelve miles away. It has been

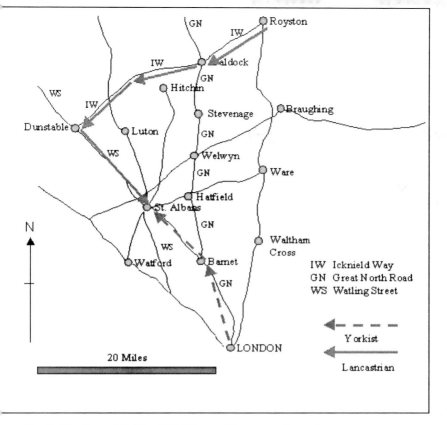

Map 3. The Second Battle of St Albans – the approach marches.

calculated that on the night of 16–17 February 1461 the moon would have been waxing towards being a half moon, so unless there was thick cloud cover, there should have been enough light for the Lancastrians to find their way. Watling Street was probably the only approach road where a night march was feasible, being straight and hedged so that troops would be unlikely to stray off. Certainly they seemed to have made good time, and by dawn on the 17th the vanguard of the Lancastrian army was on the outskirts of St Albans preparing to attack. The Yorkists appear to have been completely unaware of what had happened the previous day at Dunstable and of the imminent danger in which they now stood. According to Gregory, only one scout had given warning that Margaret's army was close at hand, 'for their prickers came not back to them to bring them tidings how near the queen was, save one who came and said that she was nine miles away.'

It may seem strange that more attention was not paid to this lone scout's warning, but during their march south Margaret's northern horde had created a swathe of destruction thirty miles wide. Their advance would have been accompanied by a stream of refugees spreading all sorts of wild and inaccurate rumours about the whereabouts of the Lancastrian army. No doubt the Yorkist commanders would have comforted themselves with the thought that they would have plenty of time to send out scouts the next morning to confirm whether or not Margaret's army was really close at hand. By boldly pressing on and marching through the night, the Lancastrians had achieved an important tactical advantage over their Yorkist opponents. Early on the 17th the Lancastrians were able to launch a surprise attack on the Yorkists from a completely unexpected direction.

The Lancastrian tactics in this campaign – the ambush at Wakefield, the outflanking march to Dunstable, the night march from Dunstable to St Albans, followed by a dawn attack – are surprisingly sophisticated for a medieval army. There were good reasons why tactics were usually simple at this time. Armies were normally an *ad hoc* collection of various groups of levies, with a stiffening of professional mercenaries, brought together for a particular campaign, and with no common standard of equipment or training. Senior commanders were appointed because of their aristocratic background and their social status. The idea of promo-

A fore-rider points out the enemy to his commander, an example of the mounted troops who failed Warwick on the night of 16–17 February 1461. *John Kliene*

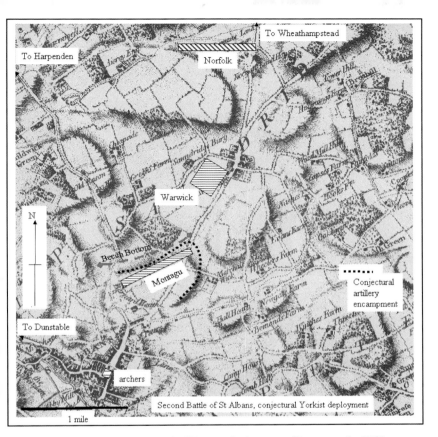

To Wheathampstead

To Harpenden

Norfolk

N

Warwick

Beech Bottom

Montagu

Conjectural artillery encampment

To Dunstable

archers

Second Battle of St Albans, conjectural Yorkist deployment

1 mile

Map 4. The Second Battle of St Albans – deployment. Shown on the 1766 Dury & Andrews map of Hertfordshire.

tion by merit or staff college training would probably have been regarded as blasphemous insults to the God-given social order. Even such simple items such as accurate, detailed maps or reliable clocks were rarely available to military commanders. On the other hand, in most armies there would have been a hard core of professional soldiers, men like Andrew Trollope and Robert Ogle. Long years of warfare in France and on the Scottish borders would have given them a great deal of experience and they certainly would have appreciated the value of ambushes and surprise attacks. It has been suggested that because the Lancastrian tactics were unusual at the Second Battle of St Albans, Queen Margaret herself may have been directing the Lancastrian army. Burne indulges in some rather fanciful speculation that Margaret may have been inspired by the exploits of her fellow countrywoman

Joan of Arc, but this does not seem very likely – and Margaret was not even present at the Battle of Wakefield. The nominal commander of the Lancastrian army was the twenty-five-year-old Henry Beaufort, 3rd Duke of Somerset, the son of Edmund Beaufort, 2nd Duke of Somerset, who had been killed in the First Battle of St Albans. Doubtless the young Somerset would have looked to an experienced professional soldier like Trollope for advice and guidance. Trollope, described by contemporaries as 'the great captain' and 'a very subtle man of war', was with the Lancastrian vanguard, and it seems likely that it was his tactical expertise that guided the Lancastrian army during this campaign. It is noteworthy that Somerset enjoyed an unbroken run of military successes once he had teamed up with Trollope after Ludford Bridge, but his success came to an abrupt end with Trollope's death at Towton.

We do not have an account of the Lancastrian command structure for the battle, but the same men commanded the same army

Henry Beaufort (1436–64), Earl of Dorset (to 1455) and 3rd Duke of Somerset (1455–64)

As the Earl of Dorset, Henry Beaufort fought at the first battle and was badly wounded – but not before seeing his father killed. He quickly had to become the Lancastrians' main battlefield commander and in 1459 teamed up with Andrew Trollope. He had an unbroken run of victories with Trollope, and an unbroken run of defeats after Trollope's death.

The Second Battle of St Albans was the apogee of his military success.

He survived Towton despite leading a desperate cavalry charge, but was finally defeated, captured and executed in 1464. Ultimately it was his personal qualities that led to success and then failure. He was a ruthless and violent man obsessed with vengeance but flawed by fecklessness and faithlessness. Alone among the Lancastrian royal dukes he was suspected of harbouring his own ambitions to take over the throne (and the queen).

(Sir) Andrew Trollope (d. 1461)

Arguably Trollope, a professional soldier from the Calais garrison, was the most able tactician on either side throughout the wars.

He joined forces with Somerset at Ludford Bridge in 1459 and then returned to England with him in 1460. He was credited with the stratagem to lure York and Salisbury out of Sandal Castle and to defeat at Wakefield. After fighting in that battle he probably masterminded the Lancastrian tactics in the run-up to, and during the course of, the Second Battle of St Albans. (Because he was still a commoner on the morning of the 17th, he could not have commanded a wing in his own right.) In recognition for his services, he was the first person to be knighted by Edward of Lancaster on the battlefield.

The nature of his perceived betrayal of the Yorkist cause in 1459 meant that he was not pardoned when Edward IV assumed the throne and he was excluded from the Yorkist settlement. Instead he was outlawed and a price put on his head. At Towton his value was recognized and rewarded by being given shared command of the vanguard with Northumberland, but he was killed in the battle.

only a few weeks later at Towton. At that battle Northumberland and Trollope (by then a knight, not just a commoner) commanded the vanguard, Somerset commanded the main battle, and Clifford the rearguard. It is a reasonable supposition to reflect this structure back on St Albans on 17 February, with the one proviso that Trollope could not have held a senior command position then.

At dawn on 17 February, Trollope and the Lancastrian vanguard crossed the site of Roman Verulamium and reached the western outskirts of St Albans at St Michael's Church. It seems likely that the rest of the ill-disciplined Lancastrian army were strung out along the road from Dunstable. Gregory certainly believed that the Lancastrian success was due to a hard core of disciplined soldiers, not the motley crowd of hangers-on who were more interested in loot and pillage: 'The substance that gained that field were household men and feed men. I ween there were not 5,000 men that fought in the queen's party, for the most part of Northern men fled away.'

The ford of the River Ver at St Michael's. *Mike Elliott*

Trollope's men crossed the River Ver by the footbridge and ford near St Michael's Church. They appear to have encountered no opposition on the road into the town and made rapid progress up to and then round the northern side of the Abbey precints via the Sallipath (now Fishpool Street), Romeland (or 'Roomland') and Church Street (now George Street). Except for the open space at Romeland, these were all narrow lanes hemmed in by buildings. Quite what the town's defences would have been here is not entirely clear, but, from reference to fighting at the other river crossing into the town at the bottom of Holywell Hill in the 1140s, it appears that the ford at St Michael's would have been in-corporated into them. Perhaps if the townspeople had been defending themselves the crossing would have been guarded, but Warwick was in command and he seems to have discounted this approach.

No resistance was encountered until Trollope and his men reached the southern end of the Market Place close to the Great Cross, or Queen's Cross. This cross was one of a series built to mark the resting places of Queen Eleanor's body as it was carried on its journey from Lincolnshire to Westminster Abbey in 1290. Suddenly the head of the Lancastrian column was hit by a storm of arrows from Yorkist archers barricaded in the buildings around the square. There are few things more demoralizing for any troops than to believe that they have achieved complete surprise, only to stumble into a well-prepared ambush. Unable to deploy in the narrow medieval streets or reply effectively to the hidden Yorkist

'Romeland' or 'Roomland' looking towards the Abbey. *With permission of St Albans Museums. From the 1907 Pageant Souvenir book – originally published 1791*

archers, the Lancastrians fell back in confusion, leaving many of their comrades dead and dying on the cobblestones of the Market Place. The Eleanor Cross has gone, but its position is still marked and in other respects this part of St Albans has changed remarkably little in five and a half centuries. The square is still dominated by the medieval Clock Tower, just as it was on that fateful February morning in 1461.

This unexpected repulse was the first crisis in the battle for the Lancastrians, but Trollope quickly took control of the situation, organizing a fresh attack up Fishpool Street and at the same time despatching scouts around the north-west edge of the town to look for an undefended entrance. The scouts soon returned and were able to report that they had discovered an unguarded lane that led into the northern part of the town.

By this time more Lancastrians would have arrived, and the chronicles talk of this phase of the attack being led by Somerset himself and a retinue of horsemen. Trollope and Somerset quickly sent a second column to enter the town by this route, which approximately followed the present-day Folly Lane and Catherine Street. This lane mostly followed round the outside of the Tonman

The 'Market Cross' from the top of the Clock Tower. The Lancastrians would have entered from George Street at the top right. The Yorkist archers staged a valiant defence of the town centre from this vantage point. *Mike Elliott*

Ditch to its north and there is a nineteenth-century report of at least parts of the ditch being 33 feet deep here.

This would have been an insurmountable passive defence against any horsemen, who would not have been able to find a route through to the back of the Market Place even had they wanted to. Another mystery, though, is why the gate across Catherine Lane was undefended, just like the ford at St Michael's. (In the first battle defended gates had successfully resisted the Yorkist attacks.) The answer was probably the same – Warwick had simply never envisaged an attack along this road. The result, whether by Trollope's military insight or by chance, was that the Lancastrians and their horsemen debouched onto the wide north–south thoroughfare (and cattle droving route) of St Peter's Street opposite the church and at the tactically most advantageous spot, splitting the Yorkist forces and with room to deploy cavalry as well as infantry.

The situation was now thoroughly confused, with one force of Lancastrians in the western end of the town, another force in the northern end of the town, Yorkist archers in between, and the rest

Folly Lane. The second Lancastrian attack found a route into St Albans here. *Mike Elliott*

of the Yorkist army further north on Bernards Heath and Sandridge. There was some fierce fighting in the centre of the town, with the Yorkist archers gradually being driven out of the buildings they had occupied. No doubt the Yorkists would have been desperately hoping for signs of a counter-attack coming to their aid from the main Yorkist army to the north, but no relief force appeared and by midday the Lancastrians were in complete control of the town.

The Yorkists were being forced by events to move their troops to fight the battle that the Lancastrians were imposing on them rather than the battle they had planned to fight. Gregory catches the moment from which there was no recovery: 'and like unwise men they broke their array and field and took another ...'.

The battle now reached a climax. The Lancastrian columns were quickly reor-

St Peter's Church and Green, 1852, before major remodelling. *Copyright unknown*

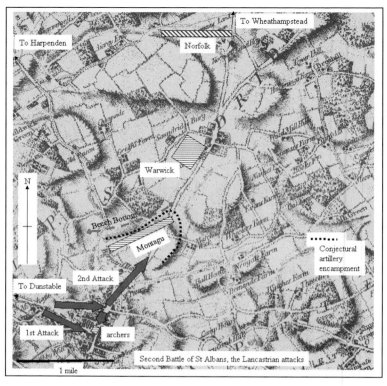

To Wheathampstead

To Harpenden

Norfolk

Warwick

N

Beech Bottom

Montagu

Conjectural
artillery
encampment

2nd Attack

To Dunstable

1st Attack

archers

Second Battle of St Albans, the Lancastrian attacks

1 mile

Map 5. The Second Battle of St Albans – action. Shown on the 1766 Dury & Andrews map of Hertfordshire.

ganized and started moving north, past St Peter's Church and on to Bernards Heath. Here they encountered Lord Montagu's division of the Yorkist army.

Whethamstede gives a vivid account of the opening stages of the battle:

> The northern men, coming to the town of the said protomartyr, and hearing that the King, with a great army and some of his lords, was lying near, immediately entered the said town, desiring to pass through the middle of it and direct their army against the King's army. However, they were compelled to turn back by a few archers who met them near the Great Cross, and to flee with disgrace to the west end of the town, where, entering by a lane which leads from

Bernards Heath: a view of one of the several remaining open spaces, looking north towards Sandridge. At the time of the second battle this whole area would have been open heath land. *Mike Elliott*

that end northwards as far as St Peter's Street, they had there a great fight with a certain small band of the people of the King's army. Then, after not a few had been killed on both sides, going out to the heath called Barnet Heath, lying near the north end of the town, they had a great battle with certain large forces, perhaps four or five thousand, of the vanguard of the King's army.

Whethamstede describes Montagu's division as the 'vanguard' – originally, of course, this force should have been the 'rearguard' of the Yorkist army, but the Lancastrian attack, coming from an unexpected direction, had placed Montagu's men at the forefront of the action. The gallant delaying action fought by the Yorkist archers in the town had given Montagu a chance to redeploy his division so that his men were facing south-west towards the town. They were probably occupying a position about half a mile to the north of St Peter's Church, astride the Sandridge Road, with their right flank resting on Beech Bottom. This would have meant that Montagu was holding a line some 900 yards long. Most of the cannons and other guns in the fortified camp would have been facing either north or north-east, and if these were to be used at all they would first have had to be dragged to new positions facing

71

towards the town. There was probably not enough time to do this, and there is a story from some seventy years later of a very large cannon ball being found in the dyke. According to Gregory, Montagu's men were still far from ready when the Lancastrians attacked:

> And before the gunners and Burgundians could level their guns they were busy fighting, and many a gun of war was provided that was of little avail or none at all ... But in time of need they could shoot not one of them, for the fire turned back on those who would shoot these things. ... They could

Light breechloading gun as might have been deployed by the Burgundians. *John Kliene*

Firing the gun – as it is meant to happen. *John Kliene*

not understand that all these devices did any good or harm except on our side with King Henry.

Unfortunately, Gregory fails to explain exactly what he means. Is he suggesting that because the Lancastrians attacked from an unexpected direction the caltrops, pavises, nets and other devices proved to be a greater hindrance to the Yorkists than to their opponents? Gregory also appears to be suggesting that not only did the Yorkist guns fail to fire, but they actually did more harm to the gunners manning them than to the enemy. One authoritative analysis of the battle states that it began to snow during the afternoon; this is not confirmed by contemporary accounts, however, and the story may have arisen because of confusion with the Battle of Towton, some six weeks later. But it was February, and if the weather was wet and unsettled it is likely that the gunpowder would have become damp, making the guns useless. Windy conditions would also have made sparks fly from the Burgundians' matches. It is easy to imagine a situation where the need to hurriedly redeploy the guns and reload them with dry powder could have led to disastrous accidents. Wet and windy conditions would also have severely hampered the use of longbows and this would help to explain how the pattern of fighting developed.

With their guns useless and many of their archers killed or captured in St Albans, Montagu's men had little choice but to engage the advancing Lancastrians in fierce hand-to-hand fighting. The fighting on Bernards Heath became a grim slugging match, with both sides anxiously waiting for reinforcements. No doubt Montagu would have been sending urgent messages to Warwick from early morning, desperately asking for the rest of the Yorkist army to be brought up in support, but the hours passed and still there was no sign of the expected reinforcements. On the Lancastrian side most of the fighting in the morning had been borne by the vanguard, but as the day wore on there was a steady flow of men arriving from Dunstable and swelling the ranks. As the odds against them lengthened, Montagu's men were steadily pushed back across Bernards Heath until eventually the pressure became too much and the Yorkists broke and fled. Montagu and Lord Berners were captured, and mounted Lancastrians were able to cut down the fleeing fugitives. One account talks of the fleeing Yorkists being caught up in thickets. The main road across the heath was used for cattle droving, suggesting a wide clear route, so the soldiers may have become disordered on this grassland and may have fled into the surrounding scrub.

As in so many battles during the Wars of the Roses, treachery – real or supposed – also played a part in deciding the outcome. By one account, at the height of the battle, one Sir Henry Lovelace, described as the captain of a company of men from Kent and commanding the vanguard of the main battle, changed sides, defecting with his men to the Lancastrians. Other accounts support the defection, but do not name Lovelace. The Burgundian historian, Jean de Waurin, writing some years after the battle, said that Lovelace had been captured at Wakefield but released by the Lancastrians when he promised to betray the Yorkist cause. Waurin describes Lovelace as one of Warwick's most trusted lieutenants, and claims that he had been put in command of the vanguard. According to Waurin, not only did Lovelace inform the Lancastrians of the Yorkist positions, but he then caused confusion in the Yorkist ranks by issuing misleading orders, and finally managed to deliver King Henry to the Lancastrians. Most historians are sceptical about Waurin's version of events. Lovelace is an obscure figure of whom little is known either before or after the battle. Perhaps significantly, neither Whethamstede nor Warwick's brother George Neville (the Chancellor of England) nor Gregory make any mention of Lovelace in their accounts of the battle. We cannot be certain, but it seems probable that the defection of Lovelace and his men was of only minor importance, though he made a convenient scapegoat for Warwick to blame in later years for the defeat.

Other accounts talk of the Kentish defection, of men breaking ranks and causing both confusion and the suspicion of treachery. It is easy to see how this could have been embellished and excused with the Lovelace story. Waurin claimed that the Yorkist defeat was caused by a deep-laid plot, similar to the situation at Northampton when Warwick had negotiated Lord Grey of Ruthyn's defection in advance. On balance, however, the chaos on Bernards Heath may owe more to the failure of Warwick's generalship than to Margaret's cunning plans.

Whethamstede clearly blames the Yorkist defeat on Warwick's failure to support Montagu's division with the rest of the Yorkist army:

> The southern men, who were fiercer at the beginning ... were broken very quickly afterwards, and the more quickly because looking back, they saw no one coming up from the main body of the King's army, or preparing to give them help, whereupon they turned their backs on the northern men and fled. ... And the northern men seeing this ... pursued them very swiftly on horseback; and catching a good many of them, ran them through with their lances.

Nothing illustrates the confusion on the Yorkist side better than the fact that in the chaos of the battle they lost control of King Henry. As Gregory stated, 'And in the midst of the battle King Henry went unto his Queen and forsook all his lords, and trust better to her party than unto his own lords.'

King Henry's tent had been pitched under an oak tree on Bernards Heath. According to some reports Henry spent the battle laughing and singing, though it's not recorded whether this was because he was delighted to see the Yorkists being defeated, or because his mental state was such that he could not understand the significance of what was happening. There are various versions of how Henry defected to the Lancastrians. As we have seen, Jean de Waurin blames the treachery of Lovelace for tricking the king. Whethamstede, however, gives a more plausible account. According to him, one Thomas Hoo (of Luton Hoo), described as a gentleman well-versed in languages and well-read in the law, approached the king and, pointing out that the Yorkist army was defeated, suggested that a messenger be sent immediately to the northern lords telling them of Henry's location. The king approved of this course of action and a messenger was sent to the Earl of

Northumberland. Several northern lords returned with the messenger and conveyed the king safely to the Lancastrian army.

We do not know when exactly this occurred, but if it happened while the battle was still raging the effect would have been a huge boost to the Lancastrians. Its consequences would have been even more important on the Yorkist side. The Yorkists up to this point in the battle still treated Henry as their legitimate king and nominal commander-in-chief of the army (however fictitious this was in practice). His sudden transition into being (nominally) the commander of the opposing army, and thus also rendering all the Yorkist combatants traitors, would have justified desertion or surrender for some – as happened at other battles in similar circumstances. It is tempting to see Henry's recapture, the Kentishmen's defection, collapse of the Yorkist front, and Montagu's and Berners' capture as linked events and not as separate episodes.

One of the unanswered questions of the battle is what exactly Warwick was doing throughout the day. Contemporary accounts are vague and it almost seems as if Warwick (along with his brother the Chancellor) was anxious to suppress any discussion of his failures during the campaign. He appears to have been taken completely by surprise by the Lancastrian dawn attack and from then on he never managed to get a grip on the battle. It seems probable that many of Warwick's men were dismayed by the fact that they had been outmanoeuvred by the Lancastrians, and the defences that they had spent days preparing were useless. No doubt they believed that the sensible thing to do was to break off the action, save what they could of the army and retreat to join the Earl of March. Certainly Davies' Chronicle refers to apparent insubordination in the Yorkist ranks: 'by indisposition of the people ... that would not be guided nor governed by their captains'.

Warwick had difficulty persuading his men to march back and support Montagu's division. When Warwick did finally get his men moving down the Sandridge Road, their morale was lowered still further by the sight of panic-stricken fugitives from Montagu's division fleeing in the opposite direction. By the time Warwick reached the battle it was too late – the whole of Montagu's division was destroyed and both Montagu and Berners were prisoners. There is one account of Warwick mounting a furious counter-attack to the south, but if this attack happened it was too little and too late. Warwick realized that he had lost both Montagu's division and the fortified area on Bernards Heath. The only sensible thing to do was to save what he could of his army.

Rallying his men, Warwick made a fighting retreat back through Sandridge, finally making a stand on the high ground to the south

Nomansland Common. Warwick made his last stand here in the dusk. *Mike Elliott*

of Nomansland common. The Lancastrians failed to attack; no doubt they preferred to pursue the fugitives from Montagu's broken division, as Whethamstede describes. In the gathering darkness Warwick was able to slip away with some 4,000 of his men. This was less than half of the army that he had commanded at the start of the battle, but at least he had managed to save something from the disaster. The failure to destroy Warwick and the remnants of his army was the biggest mistake the Lancastrians made in the battle, and one that they would later have cause to regret. However, it should be remembered that many of the Lancastrians had been continually marching or fighting since the morning of 16 February, and by the evening of 17 February they must have been exhausted.

Warwick had lost the battle because he had surrendered the initiative to the Lancastrians. He had relied on elaborate defences to win the battle for him, but at the same time he had failed to maintain contact with Margaret's army, and when the Lancastrians had launched a surprise attack from an unexpected direction he never managed to recover. By contrast, the Lancastrians had acted throughout the campaign with boldness and resolution and as a result achieved a remarkable victory.

The two armies involved in the Second Battle of St Albans were much larger than the forces involved in the first battle. Also, in the

77

second battle fighting had gone on all day from dawn to dusk, making heavy casualties inevitable, and it has been estimated that by nightfall some 2,300 men lay dead and dying either in the town or on Bernards Heath. The only Lancastrian of note who was killed in the battle was Sir John Grey of Groby. At the time the unfortunate Sir John's death probably seemed important only to his immediate family and friends. However, Sir John left behind an attractive young widow, Elizabeth Woodville, and two young sons. By an ironic twist of fate, a few years later the Yorkist King, Edward IV, fell in love with Elizabeth, insisted on marrying her, and proceeded to promote the interests of the Woodville family so that they became a counter-balance to the power of Warwick and the other Yorkist supporters. Edward's actions resulted in the Yorkists becoming bitterly divided and this eventually led to a tragic and bloody continuation of the wars.

While Warwick retreated from St Albans with the remnants of his army, the Lancastrians were celebrating their victory. King Henry was escorted to Lord Clifford's tent where he was reunited with Queen Margaret and the Prince of Wales. The king had not seen his wife and son since the Battle of Northampton some eight months before, and there were emotional scenes as he kissed and embraced them and gave thanks to God. According to Whethamstede, the reunion with his wife and son restored Henry's senses and power of rational speech (a prognosis consistent with the condition of hysterical catatonia). The queen persuaded Henry to confer knighthood upon the young prince, and the prince in turn knighted some thirty Lancastrians who had played prominent parts in the battle. Among those knighted was Trollope. He had apparently injured his foot on a caltrop, and, with a piece of preposterous false modesty, stated that this had prevented him from performing his usual heroic deeds: 'My lord, I have not deserved this for I slew no more than fifteen men. I stood still in one place and they came to me but still they stayed with me.'

King Henry and Queen Margaret together with the young prince were then escorted to the Abbey, where the monks greeted them with hymns and songs. Henry gave thanks to God at the high altar and the

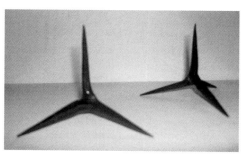

Caltrops. These are replicas but their form can be clearly seen. *With grateful thanks to Martyn Smith*

78

shrine of St Alban, before being taken to his usual quarters. Abbot Whethamstede prevailed on the king to issue a royal proclamation forbidding the Lancastrian army from looting and pillaging the town. The proclamation was ignored, however, and for a second time St Albans was brutally sacked by a victorious army.

Yorkist propaganda later claimed that the king had been left in the care of Lord Bonville and Sir Thomas Kyriell, and they, although realizing that the battle was lost, had chivalrously agreed to escort the king to Queen Margaret on the king's assurance that no harm would come to them. However, the queen, scornfully ignoring her husband's feeble protests, had both men seized and executed the following day. This story needs to be treated with some caution: both Bonville and Kyriell were experienced military commanders and it seems unlikely that their role in the battle would have been limited to looking after King Henry. It would seem more likely that they were captured with Lord Montagu during the fighting. No doubt it suited the Yorkists to portray Queen Margaret as ruthless and bloodthirsty, and King Henry as a feeble irrelevance.

After Wakefield and Mortimer's Cross it was perhaps inevitable that any leading Yorkists who had been captured would be executed, but what shocked people was the way that Margaret encouraged her son, the seven-year-old Prince of Wales, to participate, and actually sentence the prisoners to death. It is recorded that the day after the battle Queen Margaret had Bonville, Kyriell and possibly a third Yorkist commander (contemporary accounts disagree as to whether this was Thomas Kyriell's son or a certain William Gower) brought before her. Turning to her young son, she asked, 'Fair son, what manner of death shall these knights, whom ye see here, die?' The young prince, knowing what was expected of him, answered, 'Let them have their heads taken off.' The gallant old soldier Sir Thomas Kyriell is said to have scornfully replied, 'May God destroy those who have taught thee this manner of speech!' The men were all promptly taken outside and beheaded. Such incidents are not easily forgotten and perhaps it is not surprising that some ten years later, when Prince Edward was taken prisoner at the Battle of Tewkesbury, the Yorkists were equally merciless, killing him on the spot.

Montagu was spared. According to some accounts King Henry intervened to save his life because Montagu had been the king's chamberlain, but it is more likely that he was spared because Somerset's younger brother was a prisoner in Warwick's hands and Somerset feared for his life if Montagu was executed. Probably for similar reasons Berners was also spared.

King Henry may have been delighted to be reunited with his family but his return to the Lancastrian fold proved to be a political disaster for him. The behaviour of Margaret's army had shocked the whole of southern England, and by joining them Henry destroyed whatever credibility he still had. In addition, only a few weeks before Henry had solemnly agreed to the terms of the Act of Accord, naming the House of York as his rightful heirs. He had clearly broken the terms of that agreement and would inevitably be regarded as weak, inconsistent and unreliable.

While the Lancastrians celebrated their victory, Warwick was escaping to the west with some 4,000 men, the remnants of his army, and by 22 February he had joined forces with March at Chipping Norton in Oxfordshire. After their defeat at St Albans the war had reached both a military and political crisis for the Yorkists. The Lancastrian army, jubilant after the victories of Wakefield and St Albans, now stood at the gates of London. At the same time the defection of King Henry left the Act of Accord and the Yorkist political plans in ruins. As Warwick and his men retreated through the night, he must have realized that the Yorkist cause was on the verge of complete disaster.

Chapter 6

PROBLEMS WITH THE SECOND BATTLE

THE SECOND BATTLE OF St Albans has always held a particular fascination for military historians. For example, the late Alfred H. Burne in his classic, *The Battlefields of England*, published in the 1950s, wrote of the battle:

> In more ways than one this is the most remarkable battle of the Wars of the Roses – and the most tantalising. Remarkable inasmuch as it included three tactical features almost unheard of in medieval warfare – a night approach march followed by a dawn attack; a flank, instead of a frontal attack; and an army occupying a position several miles in length. Tantalising, because the records of the battle are more than usually scanty, even for that period. As a result scarcely a single historian has ventured to compile a map of the battle, and most of them slur over the inherent difficulties and problems as if they did not exist, and pass on as quickly as can decently be done to subsequent events.

It is obvious that, while there is agreement over the main sequence of events during the battle, many questions remain unanswered. The first question that we need to ask is why did the Earl of Warwick move his army to St Albans at all? If his intention was to intercept Margaret before she could reach London, then it would have made more sense to march directly up Ermine Street. We therefore have three options:

1. Warwick had received news from Royston that Margaret's army had swung westward towards Hitchin and Luton. Warwick's move to St Albans conformed to this move and ensured that his army remained between Margaret and the capital.
2. Warwick wished to avoid fighting Margaret's army until he had joined forces with Edward, Earl of March. At the same time he could not afford to simply abandon London as this would demoralize his army and probably would lead to mass desertion. By placing his army at St Albans, Warwick was in a much more convenient position to join forces with March, either via Akeman Street or Watling Street (see Map 3, p.61); he was also in position to threaten the flank and rear of the

Lancastrian army if it tried to slip past him and make a dash for London.

3. Warwick's immediate priority above all others was to safeguard London and his tactics were designed deliberately to lure Margaret away from the capital. To do this, he took King Henry with him to St Albans, knowing that Margaret would see recovering the person of the king as more important than seizing the city. For this option to work Warwick had to stay north of London, away from Margaret's immediate line of march, but still able to link up with March and to support London if either were needed. St Albans met all of these requirements.

Options 2 and 3 are not mutually exclusive and seem far more probable than option 1. Warwick left London on the morning of 12 February. If he was conforming to the movements of the Lancastrian army, it is reasonable to suppose that Margaret had swung westward from Royston on 10 February at the latest. However, we know that Margaret and her army did not reach Dunstable, only twenty-seven miles from Royston, until 16 February. Unless we are to assume that the Lancastrians wasted a week encamped in the Luton/Hitchin area, the times and distances involved are difficult to reconcile.

To understand the strategic significance of fifteenth-century St Albans for this campaign we need to look at the medieval roads which radiated out from the city (see Map 6, p.101). To the north-west ran the old Roman road of Watling Street (the modern A5) – this ran from London, via St Albans, to the West Midlands and North Wales. A few miles away at Watford was Akeman Street (the modern A41), which connected London to the South-West Midlands and South Wales. Thus it can be seen that by placing his army at St Albans, Warwick was in a good position to join forces with March when he and his army arrived from Wales. The danger was that Margaret and the Lancastrians might arrive first, swing west from their intended route to London and march directly on St Albans (as indeed the Yorkists had done in 1455).

Having reached Royston, there was only one direct route that the Lancastrians could take to reach London. This was to stay on the old Roman road of Ermine Street (the modern A10), also known as the 'Old North Road', that ran down to London via Royston, Braughing and Ware. If the Lancastrians had wanted to use the 'Great North Road' via Barnet (the modern A1000 and A1, also known as the York Road), they would have turned west much further north. They could, though, still have linked up with the Great North Road from Royston by sacrificing a day's march to join it at Welwyn, having taken Stane Street from Braughing. If the Lancastrians decided to march on westwards directly on St Albans in order to defeat Warwick's army and gain control of King Henry, they had a choice of routes. The most direct was the Stane Street route and then continuing west from Welwyn. The second most direct route was to take the ancient trackway of the Icknield Way to Baldock (the modern A505) and then join the road via Wheathampstead (then 'the King's Highway', now the B651) where it met the Icknield Way south of Hitchin. The third most direct route was to follow the route taken by the Yorkists in 1455, by marching from Ware via Hatfield to St Albans (this follows the route of the modern A414). The two less obvious, and much longer, routes were to continue on the Icknield Way to either Luton or Dunstable and turn south there (on Luton Lane or Watling Street respectively). That they took the longest and least obvious route may suggest that an outflanking rather than a head-on attack was intended, especially as it was the one route that Warwick did not seem to have prepared for as fully as the others.

In summary, Warwick moving his army to St Albans meant:

1. Warwick was in a much better position to keep the Lancastrians away from London and to join forces with March either via Watling Street or Akeman Street.
2. If he was reinforced, Warwick was in a good position to go on the offensive and move to intercept the Lancastrians either via Stane Street or the Icknield Way.
3. If the Lancastrians continued their march on London, Warwick would be in a position to threaten their flank and rear, possibly trapping them between the city walls and the Yorkist army.
4. The biggest danger was that the Lancastrians would march directly on St Albans, in order to attack Warwick's army and free King Henry before Edward could arrive with his forces. Warwick tried to safeguard against this by building elaborate field defences to the north of the town.

In the previous chapter we described the somewhat intriguing Yorkist deployments, and we now need to analyze them more closely. It is usually assumed that the Yorkists had a chain of fortified posts stretching some three and a half miles from St Albans, through Bernards Heath, the village of Sandridge, and on to Nomansland Common. Such a deployment may seem reasonable in modern times, with automatic weapons and modern communication devices available, but it would have been quite unprecedented for a medieval army. It would also make for a very curious deployment, unless Warwick was somehow certain that the attack was coming from the direction of Luton or Hitchin, and all the evidence suggests that Warwick had lost contact with the Lancastrian army and was uncertain where it was.

Local historian John Dixon has studied the battle for some years and has arrived at an alternative theory. Dixon believes that Warwick's tactics were much more conventional than is usually supposed. Probably Warwick set up a fortified camp on Bernards Heath to the north of St Albans, with his guns deployed to cover all the obvious approach routes. We have already seen that the French employed this tactic very successfully at the Battle of Castillon in 1453; the Yorkists had tried to employ a similar tactic at Ludlow in 1459, and the Lancastrians at Northampton in 1460. Bernards Heath is a plateau of high ground that dominates all the approaches to St Albans from northerly directions. It also had the advantage of a major defensive ditch or dyke, now known as Beech Bottom, which runs for over a mile along the northern edge of the Heath. Beech Bottom is a major Iron Age earthwork, probably built between 50 BC and AD 50. In places it is over 30 feet deep and 90 feet wide. Even today, after 2,000 years of erosion, overgrown with trees and bushes, and surrounded by suburban gardens, the ditch is still an impressive sight, and 550 years ago it would have been an even more formidable obstacle. The only possible weak point in this defensive position would be to the

Reconstruction of fifteenth-century encampment. *Mike Elliott*

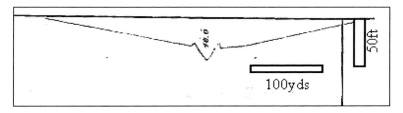

Detail from the plan presented to Parliament in 1863 with the Midland Railway Bill, showing a profile of Beech Bottom where it would be intersected by the railway. *Plan attached to the Midland Railway Bill 1863*

south-west in the direction of St Albans. Warwick guarded against this by garrisoning the town with a strong detachment of archers, and in any case the south-west must have seemed the least likely direction in which to expect a Lancastrian attack. It can be seen, therefore, that Bernards Heath would have been an ideal location for a fortified artillery encampment. No doubt Warwick would have hoped that the Lancastrians would wear themselves out with a frontal attack on formidable field fortifications and novel weaponry. Warwick could then have completed his victory with a devastating counter-attack on an exhausted and demoralized enemy.

Admittedly, there is a degree of conjecture about this theory, but it is far more logical than the oft-quoted suggestion that Warwick's field defences stretched almost four miles from St Albans to Nomansland Common. Confusion probably arises about the location of the Yorkist defences, because the Yorkist army was encamped along the road from St Albans to Nomansland Common. This would have enabled the Yorkists to spread out to forage in the surrounding area. We need to remember that the Yorkists were camped for four days in cold and wet February conditions, so shelter and firewood were of great importance. We know that Warwick had placed an outpost in Dunstable, twelve miles to the north-west of St Albans on Watling Street. It can be assumed that Warwick would also have placed similar outposts to the north and east of St Albans, ready to give a timely warning of any possible Lancastrian advance. The probability is, therefore, that Warwick's army were encamped along the road from St Albans and Sandridge, ready to advance north or east if reinforced by March's army, but also ready to withdraw into their fortified camp on Bernards Heath if their outposts warned of Margaret's approach.

Yet another of the many mysteries of this campaign is why it took March so long to join forces with Warwick. Two weeks had

The grim face of the 1461 campaign: Lionel, Lord Welles (1406–61) was with Margaret at St Albans and then Towton, where he was killed. *By kind permission of St Oswald's Church, Methley. Photograph: Robert Burley and Kate Fordham*

passed since the Battle of Mortimer's Cross, and if March had moved quickly he could have reinforced Warwick in time for the Second Battle of St Albans. It is a question which has long puzzled historians. The late H. T. Evans in his book, *Wales and the Wars of the Roses*, even speculated that March may have deliberately delayed joining Warwick in the hope that if Warwick was defeated it would make it easier for March to make himself leader of the Yorkist faction and lay claim to the throne. This theory does not seem very likely – there would have been no way that March could be sure of the exact outcome of the battle. If Warwick had defeated the Lancastrians without March's assistance, it would have confirmed Warwick's position as the dominant force in English politics; alternatively, if Warwick had been killed and his army utterly destroyed, it could have been fatal to the Yorkist cause. Neither of these outcomes would have served March's interests.

The fact is that March, later to become King Edward IV, was the most successful general of the Wars of the Roses, but his string of victories – Mortimer's Cross 1461, Towton 1461, Empingham (also known as Losecoat Field) 1470, Barnet 1471, and Tewkesbury 1471 – tend to hide the fact that on several occasions he made serious strategic errors and underestimated the opposition that he faced. February 1461 appears to have been one of those occasions. Too complacent after his victory at Mortimer's Cross, March failed to appreciate the danger that faced Warwick and he was too cautious about the possible continued Lancastrian danger in the west. He wasted two vital weeks when he should have been marching to join Warwick's army. Edward IV may have been unstoppable on the battlefield, but the suspicion remains that a better strategist or a more astute politician would not have had to fight so many battles in the first place.

86

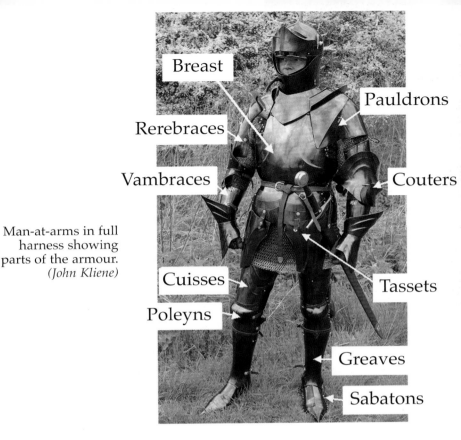

Breast

Pauldrons

Rerebraces

Vambraces

Couters

Man-at-arms in full
harness showing
parts of the armour.
(John Kliene)

Cuisses

Tassets

Poleyns

Greaves

Sabatons

The red and white cherry trees in Sandridge Road.   *(Peter Burley)*

The Earl of Warwick's men, wearing their red liveries and badges of the Bear and Ragged Staff, advance through the medieval market place, while the 'Kingmaker' raises his visor to greet the Duke of York. York, his standard bearer beside him, is indicating in the direction of the Castle Inn, scene of the Duke of Somerset's last stand, and the Abbey towers over the proceedings as it still does today. (*Graham Turner, Studio 88*)

The 1461 campaign was probably Sir John Howard's first, serving his kinsman the Duke of Norfolk – he later inherited the title and was killed at Bosworth. *(By kind permission of His Grace The Duke of Norfolk, Arundel Castle)*

1. At ease

2. Take a ball

3. Ramming

4. Priming

5. Check the match

6. Aim

7. Fire

Handgunner sequence. *(Peter Shepherd, John Kliene)*

Chapter 7

THE AFTERMATH

THE SIX WEEKS THAT followed the Second Battle of St Albans were a crucial period in the Wars of the Roses. They witnessed one of the dramatic turning points in British history, yet to most observers in the immediate aftermath of the Earl of Warwick's defeat it must have seemed that the issue was settled, and the Lancastrians had only to march into London to restore King Henry to the throne and complete their victory.

News of the Lancastrian victory at St Albans reached London on Wednesday, 18 February, and immediately plunged Londoners into a state of panic and dismay. No one was sure what had happened to Warwick; various rumours claimed that he was a prisoner of Queen Margaret or that he had fled to Calais. It was clear that nothing now stood between the victorious Lancastrian army and London. Most Londoners were strongly pro-Yorkist and they dreaded the arrival of Margaret's army. They looked on the north of England as a violent and lawless area, whose impoverished inhabitants regarded their more prosperous southern neighbours with envy and jealousy. For weeks Londoners had been hearing reports of Margaret's northern army pillaging and plundering as it moved south; now it seemed there was nothing to prevent London, 'the wealthiest city in Christendom', from being sacked and pillaged. Shops were closed, the streets were deserted, and armed militia patrolled the city walls. People buried their valuables and barricaded themselves in their homes.

Many of those who could afford to fled overseas. One such was prosperous London citizen Philip Malpas, who had already had his house sacked during Jack Cade's rebellion some eleven years before, and who now fled to Antwerp to await safer times. In Baynard's Castle the Duke of York's widow, Cicely Neville, feared for the safety of her two youngest sons, George and Richard. Cicely had already lost a husband and a son in the disaster at Wakefield and she now sent the two younger boys to safety overseas at the court of the Duke of Burgundy. Cicely herself stubbornly refused to leave, stating that she would await the arrival of her eldest son, Edward, Earl of March. Both George and Richard survived to play important roles in the later stages of the Wars of the Roses: George would become Duke of Clarence, and Richard would become Duke of Gloucester and eventually be crowned King Richard III.

The Mayor and Aldermen of London were in an unenviable position. They were caught between the Lancastrian army on one side and the pro-Yorkist London mob on the other. They tried to negotiate a surrender which would not result in London being sacked and pillaged. Their first step was to send a delegation to Queen Margaret. It consisted of the Dowager Duchess of Buckingham, the Dowager Duchess of Bedford, Lady Scales and a large group of clergy. The delegation was instructed to promise King Henry and Queen Margaret that the London city gates would be opened and they would be able to enter London unopposed, as long as they were only accompanied by a small disciplined force, and any looting and pillaging was avoided.

At this moment a bold and decisive move by the Lancastrians would probably have captured London and possibly have won the war, but for some reason Margaret hesitated. The Lancastrian army was probably exhausted and overextended after a battle in which, even though they had won, they had been badly mauled, and they may well have lacked the physical resources needed to make a serious assault on London after their recent exertions. The queen may also have belatedly realized the harm that was being done to the Lancastrian cause by the behaviour of her ill-disciplined army, and a bloodbath in the streets of London would hardly endear her young son to his future subjects. In reaching any decision Margaret would have had to consider her somewhat ambiguous position within the Lancastrian army. In medieval society it was not acceptable for a woman to be seen commanding an army, and although she had great influence in private, in public at least she would have to defer to the young Duke of Somerset, who nominally commanded the Lancastrian army. Somerset would have been expected to listen to professional advisers, such as Sir Andrew Trollope. Further complicating matters was the

The Attrition of the Commanders

Unlike in modern wars, the rate of attrition was greater in the Wars of the Roses the higher up the command structure. Of the ten or so men who had identifiable senior command roles in the first battle, only one died in his bed, and all the active Lancastrian commanders were liquidated.

presence of King Henry, who no doubt would have been urging moderation. This was a complex command structure, and reaching agreement on any important decision must have been difficult. Eventually it was decided to withdraw the bulk of the Lancastrian army back to Dunstable, while a small, picked force of 400 men marched to Barnet ready to enter London.

In exchange for this restraint on the part of the Lancastrians, the London authorities were expected to make a public declaration that March was a rebel and a traitor. London was also expected to supply the Lancastrian army with supplies of food and drink, and money to pay the men. The money was particularly important, as many of the men in the Lancastrian army believed that they had the right to loot and plunder the country south of the Trent in lieu of regular pay. They were going to feel cheated if they were not allowed to plunder London.

A letter from an Italian merchant who was resident in London gives a vivid picture of the atmosphere in the city at this time. The merchant records that, in order to avoid any violence, the city authorities issued a proclamation instructing Londoners to stay in their homes and act peacefully when the king and queen entered London with their forces. However, within a matter of hours the mood changed – rumours began circulating that York was marching on London with an Irish army and at the same time March was reported to be approaching with a Welsh army! Mobs of armed Londoners were soon roaming the streets proclaiming their determination to hold the city against Queen Margaret. It is interesting to note that two months after Wakefield, many Londoners apparently still believed that York was alive and might be marching to their aid. The situation did calm down temporarily, and on 22 February the city authorities arranged for a convoy of carts loaded with supplies to be sent to the Lancastrian army. The convoy also included a shipment of money to help Queen Margaret pay her men. However, when the convoy got to Cripplegate a mob of Londoners refused to open the gates and seized the supplies for themselves. Somewhere in the confusion the money also disappeared. Gregory remarked, 'I wot not how it departed – I trow the purse stole the money.'

While the citizens of London anxiously awaited their fate, Warwick was retreating with the tired, defeated and demoralized remnants of his army towards Oxfordshire. Warwick had much to consider: clearly the most urgent task was to assemble an army capable of facing Margaret's northern host, and the only way to achieve that was for Warwick to join forces with Edward's army from Wales. As well as the immediate military problem there was also the political problem of finding a way to rally support behind

Museum of London plaque at Cripplegate, from an eighteenth-century engraving, showing medieval Cripplegate as it appeared after rebuilding in 1491 and alteration in 1663. *Peter Burley*

London city wall near Cripplegate, where the Lancastrians sought access to the city. *Peter Burley*

the Yorkist cause. Warwick had been opposed to York's attempt to seize the throne the previous October, but he must have realized that the Act of Accord, keeping Henry VI on the throne but recognizing York as the rightful heir, was always going to be a clumsy and improbable compromise. To have any credibility at all, the Act needed at least the tacit support of King Henry and it was obvious after St Albans that this no longer existed. In any case it was widely recognized that Henry was totally unfit to rule the country – hence the Lancastrians' increasing emphasis on the role of the young Edward, Prince of Wales, who represented the future for the House of Lancaster. The solution was obvious: Warwick decided that Henry had to be deposed and March proclaimed king. March appeared to be the ideal candidate – of royal descent, over 6 feet 2 inches tall, handsome and charismatic, he had leapt to fame with his victory at Mortimer's Cross. We cannot be sure when Warwick made this momentous decision. It is possible that Warwick had already decided before St Albans that Henry was no longer of much value to the Yorkist cause, and this was why Warwick was able to face March having lost the King of England on the battlefield of St

Albans. Certainly by the time Warwick met March in the Cotswolds on 22 February, he had decided on the necessary course of action. It must have been an uncomfortable meeting for Warwick. Previously he had always filled the role of the experienced politician and the successful military commander, while the younger March had been his protégé. Now the roles had been reversed: with the death of his father at Wakefield and his victory at Mortimer's Cross, March had clearly established himself as leader of the Yorkist party, while Warwick had to try and explain away his humiliating defeat at St Albans. According to some accounts, the first thing that March asked was, 'Where is the King?' To which Warwick smoothly replied, 'But *you* are the King.'

No doubt March would have needed little persuading that he should now claim the throne. The Yorkists must have been heartened by the startling news that Queen Margaret and the Lancastrians had not yet been able to capture London. March and Warwick decided to march immediately on London and relieve the city.

Meanwhile in London the mood of defiance was encouraged by the rumours that Warwick was still alive and had joined forces with March, and that their combined army was marching on the city. By Monday, 23 February these rumours were beginning to harden into fact. When the small Lancastrian force at Barnet advanced to the city gates they were refused admission. When another small Lancastrian force reached Westminster they received such rough treatment from the Londoners that they quickly withdrew. By 25 February the Lancastrian scouts had confirmed the news, Warwick and March had joined forces, and their combined army would soon reach London. The Lancastrians faced a difficult choice. Their army was ill-prepared to fight another battle. Cheated of the opportunity to plunder London, many of their men had already deserted and were making their way home with whatever booty they could carry. Margaret and the Lancastrian leadership realized that they had to retreat back to the north of England to reorganize their army and raise new recruits before they faced March and Warwick for the decisive battle. It must have been a bitter pill to swallow, to have to retreat with London almost in their grasp, but soon the Lancastrian army had started its long weary march back to Yorkshire.

On Thursday, 26 February the Yorkist advance guard reached London, and on the following day Warwick and March entered the city in triumph. The time had now arrived to implement the Yorkist plan to depose King Henry and proclaim March the rightful King of England. Warwick must have been keenly aware that York's clumsy and abortive attempt to make himself king the previous

October had been a dismal failure, and he would have been determined to ensure that there was no repetition of that fiasco.

On Sunday, 1 March a great assembly of London citizens and Yorkist soldiers was gathered at St John's Fields in Clerkenwell. March was kept well out of sight, and the crowd were addressed by Warwick's younger brother, George Neville, the Lord Chancellor. Neville reminded the crowd that Henry was really a usurper – he was only king because his grandfather had seized the throne by force some sixty years before. Feeble-minded Henry's reign had been a dreadful failure, with violent dissent at home and humiliating defeats abroad. Now Henry had broken the terms of the Act of Accord, terms which he had solemnly agreed to only a few months before. By voluntarily placing himself in the power of Queen Margaret he had forfeited any remaining right to the throne. By comparison, March was an excellent young prince of royal descent, whose claim to the royal succession had already been recognized by Parliament. Neville demanded of the crowd, was Henry worthy to reign as king any longer or not? The crowd roared back their answer, 'Nay! Nay!' Then the crowd were asked if they wanted Edward, Earl of March as their king, and the crowd enthusiastically cried out, 'Yea, Yea, King Edward, King Edward!'

Warwick must have been delighted with this enthusiastic response and the next day a deputation waited on March at Baynard's Castle and offered him the crown. No doubt March had been well rehearsed, for he expressed great surprise and modestly claimed that he was not worthy of such high office. He soon, however, allowed himself to be persuaded that it was his duty to accept the crown.

On Wednesday, 4 March Edward, Earl of March was proclaimed King of England at the Cross at St Paul's. After hearing a *Te Deum* in St Paul's Cathedral, he went in solemn procession to Westminster Hall, where the royal robes were placed on him and he sat on the throne to be acclaimed by the nobles present. Everywhere Edward went he was greeted by large and enthusiastic crowds, but this could not disguise the fact that there were few nobles present to acclaim him. The only really important peers at the ceremony were Warwick, Norfolk, the Archbishop of Canterbury and the Bishops of Salisbury and Exeter. Having been acclaimed, Edward then walked to Westminster Abbey where he was presented with the crown and sceptre, and then prayed at the tomb of St Edward the Confessor.

The only thing missing from all this ceremonial pomp and splendour was the actual coronation. Edward was well aware that England now had two kings, both claiming the throne, and the issue could only be resolved on the battlefield. Until Edward had clearly and decisively defeated the Lancastrians there was little point in proceeding with an elaborate coronation. Although Edward's usurpation of the throne had been carefully stage-managed by Warwick, there is doubt that it was greeted enthusiastically by the great majority of Londoners. On 4 March an Italian living in London wrote of the 'great multitude who say that they want to be with him to conquer or die'. William Gregory recorded a contemporary rhyme: 'Let us walk in a new vineyard, and let us make a gay garden in the month of March with this fair white rose and herb, the Earl of March.'

Both Yorkists and Lancastrians tried to rally as much support as possible for what was clearly going to be a decisive battle. Edward sent proclamations to every county, demanding that he now be recognized as rightful king, and offering pardons to those who had previously supported King Henry but would now swear allegiance to him. Meanwhile from the city of York the Lancastrians were sending out letters in King Henry's name commanding all true subjects to rally to the king's standard and help crush this upstart pretender, the Earl of March.

It has been estimated that the Lancastrians had the support of nineteen peers of the realm, including many of the stalwarts of the Lancastrian cause, such as the Duke of Somerset, the Earl of Northumberland, the Earl of Wiltshire, the Duke of Buckingham, the Duke of Exeter, the Earl of Devon, and the Earl of Shrewsbury. The Lancastrian army also contained some sixty famous knights, including soldiers such as Sir Andrew Trollope. Most of the Lancastrian support came from the rural areas in the north and west of England, where traditional feudal loyalties still held sway.

Compared to the Lancastrians, the Yorkists had the support of a much smaller share of the nobility. Only eight peers backed the Yorkist cause, and as a result Edward had to rely on the support of cities like London, with its merchants, traders and small landowners. Although people may not have realized it at the time, the campaign was more than just a dynastic struggle for power; it was a clash between the old traditional feudal loyalties of the past and the new middle classes which were emerging from the wreckage of medieval England.

On 5 March Sir John Mowbray, Duke of Norfolk left London to raise men from his estates in East Anglia; three days later Warwick left to raise a force from his estates in the Midlands; on 11 March Lord Fauconberg left London with the Yorkist vanguard; and finally on 13 March Edward marched north with the main body of the army. Warwick struck the first blow. In Coventry his men captured two illegitimate sons of the Duke of Exeter. They were reported to have played a leading part in the execution of

Warwick's father, the Earl of Salisbury, after the disaster at Wakefield. Warwick wasted no time in having them both beheaded.

By Friday, 27 March the Yorkist army was assembling at Pontefract, in South Yorkshire. Edward had been joined by Warwick and Fauconberg, but they were still awaiting the arrival of Norfolk. Scouts reported that the Lancastrians had assembled an enormous army which was encamped between the villages of Saxton and Towton a few miles to the north. The Battle of Towton is often described as the biggest battle ever fought on British soil, but considerable uncertainty exists about the actual size of the armies. We have the usual wild exaggerations by some medieval chroniclers, but if we ignore these, then a realistic estimate would suggest that some 30,000 Lancastrians were facing a Yorkist army of some 25,000 men. With over 50,000 men present on the battlefield, Towton was undoubtedly the largest battle of the Wars of the Roses.

The advantage of superior numbers lay with the Lancastrians, particularly as Norfolk's division had not yet joined Edward. However, Edward was reluctant to delay his advance and he despatched John Radcliffe, Lord Fitzwalter to seize the bridge over the River Aire at Ferrybridge. Fitzwalter's men found the bridge partially destroyed and promptly set about repairing it, but unknown to them, their presence at the bridge had been discovered by the Lancastrians. At dawn on the 28th Fitzwalter's men were suddenly attacked and overrun by a Lancastrian raiding force led by Lord Clifford. In the confusion Fitzwalter and many of his men were killed and the panic-stricken survivors fled south to Pontefract crying that the whole Lancastrian army was upon them. Warwick helped rally the Yorkists by dramatically killing his horse in front of his men and announcing that he was not going to ride away but would either conquer or die on the spot. There can be no doubt that Warwick's reputation had suffered badly because of the Second Battle of St Albans and the rumours that he had retreated leaving his brother and the Yorkist left wing to its fate. Is this the reason that he felt the need to make such a melodramatic gesture? In fact there was no need for such theatrical drama – Clifford was only leading a small raiding force and they advanced no further south than the river. By midday, Edward had rallied the Yorkist army and advanced to Ferrybridge, where they found that Clifford's men had destroyed the repairs to the bridge and were defiantly holding the north bank of the river. While the main Yorkist force tried to fight their way over the ruined bridge, Fauconberg was sent with a mounted force to outflank the Lancastrians by crossing the River Aire a few miles upstream at Castleford. As soon as his scouts reported that Fauconberg was across the river and threatening to cut off his retreat, Clifford ordered his men to fall back on the main Lancastrian army. However, he had left it too late. Fauconberg caught up with Clifford at the village of Dintingdale. In the resulting skirmish Clifford's force was destroyed and Clifford was killed. The death of Clifford, who had been nicknamed 'bloody Clifford' for the murder of the Earl of Rutland after the Battle of Wakefield, was particularly satisfying for the Yorkists.

The following morning the two armies deployed, facing each other in the fields between the villages of Saxton and Towton. It was a cold, misty morning and as the armies waited, across the frozen fields they could hear the distant sound of church bells reminding them that this was a Sunday. In fact it was Palm Sunday, 29 March 1461, a date destined to be remembered as one of the bloodiest in British history. Neither King Henry nor Queen Margaret was present on this momentous day. They had been persuaded to stay safely in the city of York with their young son while Somerset and other Lancastrian nobles fought the battle for them.

By mid-morning the weather had worsened, bringing snow and a wind that blew the snow towards the Lancastrians. Fauconberg, an experienced soldier, quickly seized the opportunity that this presented. He ordered the Yorkist archers to advance a short distance and start shooting into the Lancastrian ranks at extreme range. He then ordered the archers to fall back a few paces. When the Lancastrians replied, shooting volley after volley into the wind, their arrows fell harmlessly in front of the Yorkist position. With the snow blowing in their faces, the Lancastrians failed to see that they were shooting their arrows to no purpose. To add insult to injury, Fauconberg ordered the Yorkist archers forward once more and, picking up the Lancastrian arrows, they were able to shoot them back at their original owners! As Somerset gradually realized that the Lancastrians were getting the worst of the archery duel, he ordered his army to advance and close with the Yorkists. Within a few minutes the two front ranks were engaged in ferocious hand-to-hand fighting. The battle raged for hours, with the casualties on both sides steadily mounting. Despite heroic efforts by Edward and Warwick, sheer weight of numbers began to tell, and step by step the Yorkists were being steadily pushed back. By mid-afternoon the situation was critical, but it was at this moment that Norfolk's division suddenly appeared on the battlefield and fell on the Lancastrian left flank. The dramatic appearance of these fresh reinforcements was as demoralizing to the Lancastrians as it was encouraging to the Yorkists. The tide began to turn and now it was the Lancastrians who were slowly being pushed back. As the afternoon wore on the exhausted and dejected Lancastrian army began to disintegrate as more and more of its men sought safety in flight.

To the west of the battlefield the fields sloped down to the River Cock and the Lancastrian right wing found themselves being driven down the muddy slopes towards the river. Men tried desperately to wade across the swollen stream, only to be trampled underfoot by the great mass of fugitives behind them. In some places there were so many dead that the stream became choked and the bodies created a macabre bridge, so that later fugitives were able to cross the river without getting their feet wet. The site where these scenes occurred is still known as the 'Bloody Meadow'. The Lancastrian casualties were appalling. Among them were the Earl of Northumberland, the Duke of Buckingham and Lord Dacre of Gilsland.

An important Lancastrian casualty was Sir Andrew Trollope. Only a few weeks before he had been hailed as the hero of the Second Battle of St Albans and knighted by the young Prince of Wales. Now he was just one of the many thousands who lay dead and dying in the freezing muddy fields between Saxton and Towton. An experienced professional soldier, Trollope had played an important part in the Lancastrian victories of Wakefield and St

Albans. The Lancastrians could ill afford to lose Trollope's experience and tactical skills. In the days following the battle two more Lancastrian noblemen, the Earl of Devon and the Earl of Wiltshire, were both captured and executed. Estimates of the total number of casualties vary from 9,000 to 28,000. Even if we accept the lower figure as being the more realistic, Towton undoubtedly deserves its reputation as one of the bloodiest battles ever fought on British soil.

As soon as they heard the dreadful news of the battle, Margaret, Henry and their young son hurriedly left York and fled north to Scotland. For Margaret it must have seemed that the wheel had come full circle. Everything that had been gained at Wakefield and St Albans had been lost, and once again, as after the Battle of Northampton, Margaret found herself a hunted fugitive.

Edward and Warwick entered York in triumph. Warwick's younger brother, Lord Montagu, a prisoner since the Second Battle of St Albans, was discovered alive and released. The rotting heads of York, Rutland and Salisbury were carefully removed from above the Micklegate Bar and given a proper burial. Edward wasted no time in replacing them with the severed heads of Lancastrian noblemen.

The Battle of Towton was decisive. The reign of Henry VI was finished, and Edward was able to return to London in triumph and arrange for his coronation. England had a new king and the Yorkist defeats at Wakefield and St Albans had been avenged.

Chapter 8

ST ALBANS AND BERNARDS HEATH AT THE TIME OF THE BATTLES

THIS CHAPTER DESCRIBES the town in which the fighting took place in 1455 and again in 1461. It explains some of the features of the battlefields and places St Albans in the wider context of the Wars of the Roses.

The earliest settlement was at Verlamion, a Celtic tribal centre to the south-west of the subsequent Roman city of Verulamium and in the area now known as Gorhambury. Its only remains today are a number of earthworks associated with it, the most enduring and remarkable of which is now known as Beech Bottom. This dyke ran out from Verlamion to the north-east. The dyke is a massive construction 30 feet deep with a rampart along the top of each bank. Beech Bottom played no role in the first battle, but Warwick seems to have tried to incorporate it into his field fortifications prior to the second battle.

The next settlement was the Roman city of Verulamium. Its fame rested on the martyrdom of Alban in AD 209. Alban was the first Christian martyr in Britain, or 'protomartyr', and the later St Albans was often referred to simply as 'the town of the protomartyr'. The only English pope (Nicholas Breakspear, a local man) ruled that St Albans was the oldest site of Christian worship in Britain and its Abbey, accordingly, the premier Abbey of the country. The Abbey always enjoyed royal patronage, and, in return, always supported the Crown in times of trouble.

The name of St Albans

St Albans is the modern spelling and dates specifically to the Act of Parliament creating it a city in 1879, when the apostrophe was omitted. Previously it had been known as St Alban's (as in Shakespeare) or St Alban's Bury. There are any number of medieval variations on the spelling, the commonest being St Alboyne's.

The Roman city was built on the south side of the River Ver and is not, therefore, the direct forebear of the modern city on the north side. By the time of the battles, Verulamium was a grassy ruin and most of its brick and stone had been quarried to build the Saxon and then Norman Abbeys. It might still have been an unattractive obstacle for an army to try to cross against opposition, especially as the Abbey also maintained an extensive system of water meadows, fish ponds and watercress beds along the river. In the event, none of the armies tried to pass through it in either battle.

The third settlement was the Saxon burgh of Kingsbury (also sometimes referred to as 'Kingsbury Castle'). Traditional interpretation has been that it was directly opposite Verulamium on the north side of the river. Recent archaeology, however, has placed it further west inside the bounds of Verulamium and centred on the present-day St Michael's village. It became a burgh under King Alfred (although not a royal burgh). Its famous huge fishpond, from which Fishpool Street takes its name, had long been drained by the time of the battle. The traditional location of Kingsbury meant that it was assumed that the western parts of the Tonman Ditch, of which more below, marked the boundary and defences of the Saxon town. This is now considered unlikely. The archaeological relocation of Kingsbury does create a naming problem, because Kingsbury is the name now given to the plateau of higher ground between the Abbey and St Michael's. For ease of reference to the modern townscape, the name Kingsbury will be used for the area now called by that name.

The Abbey itself can be accounted the fourth settlement and it stands on the promontory of Holmhurst Hill above the River Ver across from the site of the Roman city. Bede records a church or shrine to St Alban dating back to the time of the Saxon conversion to Christianity, and perhaps even a direct survival of a Roman church. The Abbey in its exact present location was founded in 793 by King Offa. It became the nucleus for a settlement in the lands immediately surrounding its precincts. This settlement became the Abbey Parish and the Saxon town.

The Abbey had been raided by the Danes and was perilously close to the boundary with Danelaw at Wheathampstead. To guard against this, fortifications seem to have been built round the Saxon settlement. These would have consisted of an earthen ditch and bank, the bank surmounted by a palisade or hedge. There were many surviving Roman and Saxon features which may have been incorporated into this earthwork. The Abbey precinct itself was also then enclosed with a wall that was earth and cob until the twelfth century and crenellated masonry thereafter. To the west of the Abbey there was a deliberate open space. This is now Romeland (from the original 'Roomland') and was the site of seasonal markets and fairs. There was a gate called Bone Gate across Fishpool Street (then called the Sallipath) at the western end of Romeland.

The Abbey quickly became one of England's most visited places of pilgrimage up to the time of the battles. By the fifteenth century the Abbey and its precincts had been developed to become the size of a small town in its own right. The complex housed 100 monks and a huge staff of servants. It was a massive development of masonry buildings and it completely dominated the area.

In the thirteenth and fourteenth centuries there had been periods of armed hostility between the Abbey and the town. The combination of local unrest and national civil wars led to the precincts becoming a crenellated fortress and, for a time, garrisoned by foreign mercenaries to protect the monks against their own parishioners. This meant that militarily the Abbey could have played the role of a castle in the middle of the town. The still surviving Abbey Gateway would grace any medieval fortress and the now demolished structure of Waxhouse Gate was also part of the defences. That said, there were complaints by the fifteenth century of the wall being in a ruinous state in places.

The way events unfolded, neither army in either battle attempted to garrison and hold the Abbey prior to the engagements or to pass through its grounds. This was most likely because of the risk of the accusation of sacrilege. Another reason for not putting the Abbey at risk was that the west end of the complex contained stabling and apartments for visiting royalty and the royal household. Henry VI stayed there, and Margaret installed the Lancastrian court there after her victory in 1461. The Abbey was at risk, though, from pillage after the battles, particularly after the second.

It is the fifth and final settlement – of the parts of St Albans north of the Abbey – that formed the greater part of the urban battlefields. This was a Norman development, but accommodated within Abbot Ulsinus' original town plan of 948. This 948 plan still gives central St Albans its current size and shape. The boundaries associated with the medieval town need to be unravelled to understand some of the references in the chronicles relating to the battles. Ulsinus established the parish boundaries in 948, but the Norman town outgrew the Abbey Parish and a new (civic) town boundary was delineated in 1327 to take in the new development. This boundary lasted until 1832 and is best shown on the 1634 'Hare' map. The town's defences (the Tonman Ditch) mostly follow this 1327 town boundary, but some parts of the town lay

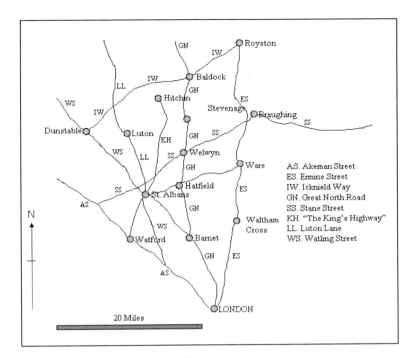

Map 6. The medieval road network.

outside the ditch. This means that some of the Bars into the town lay on its boundary (such as Sopwell Lane Bar at Keyfield), but some were inside it (such as Bowgate outside St Peter's Church).

The shrine of St Alban lay at the centre of Ulsinus' plan (and the 1327 boundary). Chapels, which also served as parish churches for the surrounding areas, were founded in 948 at three nearly equidistant points on the three main roads giving access to the shrine (on Watling Street at either end of where it came into Verulamium, catching pilgrims from the east, west and south, and one on the northern road into the town after the junction of the roads that would be known by the time of the battles as 'the King's Highway' and as Luton Lane).

The main north–south road through the town was St Peter's Street, running on into Holywell Hill with St Peter's Church at the north end and the River Ver at the south where it ran on to St Stephen's (up St Stephen's Hill). There was no equivalent east–west thoroughfare through the town until the nineteenth century (when London Road was joined up with Verulam Road).

In the fifteenth century Watling Street had long been diverted onto local roads and the main road from London via Barnet came into the town along Sopwell Lane and ended at Holywell Hill. This road layout affected the course of the battles, because all the assaults on the town were on the east–west axis on narrow constricted roads. The tide of battle turned on both occasions at the point when armies debouched onto the wider north–south thoroughfare of St Peter's Street and Holywell Hill.

The 1327 town was divided between three parishes. The Abbey

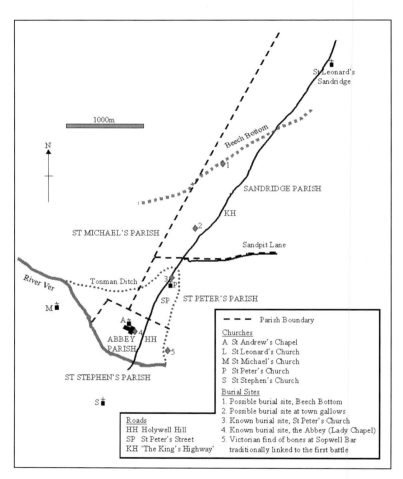

Map 7. Diagrammatic map of medieval St Albans, showing churches, parishes and confirmed or conjectural burial sites.

precincts and their environs eastwards to the Tonman Ditch were the Abbey Parish, roughly coterminous with the Saxon town, and whose parish church was St Andrew's Chapel which rested against the north-west side of the Abbey's nave. (It was demolished by 1543 and the parish functions transferred to the Abbey as part of the post-Reformation settlement.) The Norman town then expanded northwards into St Peter's Parish (from a line roughly north of the market place/Shropshire Lane) and westwards into St Michael's Parish. There were, therefore, two parish churches within the 1327 boundary and the Tonman Ditch, and this means that caution is needed when interpreting contemporary references to parish churches to be sure to distinguish between St Andrew's and St Peter's. There was, however, an arrangement by the time of the battles between St Andrew's and St Peter's that normal town burials would be in St Peter's graveyard and no longer inside the Abbey precincts. This was significant for the eventual resting place of the fallen in both battles.

One feature of the Abbey Parish of relevance to the first battle was that the property holdings east of the Abbey along Holywell Hill were very distinctive. They were all long narrow plots running all the way back from the main road to the Tonman Ditch. They typically had just one substantial building, fronting Holywell Hill, and gardens and outbuildings in the ground up to the ditch.

St Peter's Street and the land either side of it and within the Tonman Ditch became the commercial district, with a weekly cattle market and the still thriving general market. The current pattern of Wednesday and Saturday markets was confirmed and formalized by a Charter of Edward VI's reign, but is probably much older.

The Market Place lay just north of the Abbey, opposite Waxhouse Gate, which was then an imposing fortified tower. The square there boasted two important features. These were an Eleanor Cross (until the mid-1630s) and the town's own 'curfew tower' (erected 1403–12). Originally the land north of the curfew tower had been an open trading area, but by the fifteenth century permanent shops and the present street plan were starting to replace the market stalls. The alleyways here are named after the produce sold on the stalls and their layout reflects the original position of the stalls rather than town planning. There were a number of ponds in St Peter's Street where the cattle could be watered, the largest occupying the triangle of land now in front of the old Town Hall. (This town hall encroaches into the medieval northern part of the Market Place. The old law courts at the back of it stand on the site of the medieval Moot Hall and a timber yard.) There were also a remarkable number of hostelries in the town, a

French Row, off the Market Place. *R. Lydekker,* Cambridge County Geographies: Hertfordshire, *Cambridge University Press, 1909*

tradition the city maintains to this day.

The buildings in the town, even the substantial structures, were timber framed on a foundation of clunch. One reason for this was the lack of good local building stone – the Norman Abbey was built of brick from Verulamium and stone from Caen in Normandy. The other reason was that the Abbey positively discouraged any constructions that could potentially rival its own. (The only real exception was the clock tower, whose construction had been a major triumph of laity over clergy.) The effect of all this was of a town where densely packed two- and three-storey buildings alternated with open spaces. Attacking armies found that they could make no progress when they were hemmed into well-defended streets, but that once they could deploy into the open spaces they could carry the day. This happened when Warwick's men broke into the Market Place in the first battle and when the Lancastrians could deploy south and north along the wide market spaces of St Peter's Street in the second.

There is no official record of the population between the Doomsday Book (500 people in 1086) and the first census (nearly 8,000 people in 1801). Meticulous research from parish records, though, has shown that the permanent civil population from the late Middle Ages to the eighteenth century stayed at about 3,000 people. To these should be added the several hundred people asso-

Looking up George Street, Trollope's line of attack, showing its steepness and the medieval townscape. *Mike Elliott*

ciated with the Abbey up to 1539, the people coming in to work or sell their wares from the surrounding countryside, and the thousands of pilgrims when they were there. (There is no indication, though, that pilgrims were present in any numbers during either battle nor that any were caught up in the fighting.)

The point of having a town here at all was the shrine to St Alban in the Abbey. The shrine that can be seen today was first built in 1320 and in its heyday it would have been truly magnificent. It was embellished with Purbeck marble and was painted red, blue and gold. There was a silk canopy above it and it would have been adorned with gifts and jewels. There was so much of value on display that specially recruited Abbey servants kept permanent watch on it from an oaken viewing gallery, which is also still there today. Only the rich and famous, though, were allowed right up to the shrine, where they could reach in through holes to touch the actual bones. Most people would have had to adore it from a distance.

St Albans was an important and attractive target during many of the civil wars in the Middle Ages. There was fighting round the Abbey during the wars in the 1140s in King Stephen's reign. The town was garrisoned and treated harshly during and after the civil wars in King John's reign. 'French Row' is said to owe its name to the French troops quartered there when Louis the Dauphin was

The Shrine of St Alban, St Albans Abbey. *By kind permission of St Albans Abbey. Photograph: John Kliene*

hoping to become King of England. There was further unrest during the wars with the barons in Henry III's reign and at the beginning of Edward I's.

In the Wars of the Roses it was the most disputed and marched-through town in England. Following Philip Haigh's account of the campaigns in the wars, it can be deduced that apart from the two battles themselves – and no other town was fought over twice – armies passed through on five further occasions. (These were Yorkists en route to Northampton in 1460, Yorkists en route to Towton in 1461, Lancastrians under Warwick en route to Edgecote in 1469, and both armies in the preliminaries to Barnet in 1471.) St Albans was not on the most important roads to the north, so the most likely attraction was that it could have billeted a small army and was an ideal place for revictualling and gathering local reinforcements. In addition, any royalty present could always rely on a comfortable bed in the Abbey.

The town did, however, try to protect itself. There had been Saxon defences against the Danes, and in the 1140s an earthen ditch and bank fortification was formalized round the whole of the then town and named the Tonman Ditch. This ditch was owned and maintained by the Abbey and was also known as the 'Monks' Ditch'. St Albans was known in the twelfth century as 'little London' for the reputed strength of its defences. The ditch was strengthened again in Henry III's reign. The ditch seems to have exploited existing boundary features where they could readily be incorporated. These different origins and phases of construction also suggest that it may not have been of a uniform design.

Two of the eastern parts of the ditch have been described in some detail. From medieval records we know that the stretch of ditch from Cock Lane to Shropshire Lane housed the town's archery butts and was maintained by the Abbey's almoner. It was deep enough to contain misdirected arrows and wide enough to double up as a roadway, which it now is as Marlborough and Upper Marlborough Roads. A section at Keyfield was excavated in 1961 and showed the ditch there to have been 20 feet wide and 15 feet deep. Remains of the ditch can still be made out in Upper Marlborough Road and in Keyfield. On the western side of the town in modern Kingsbury there was a nineteenth-century report of a 33-foot-high bank (i.e. from bottom of ditch to top of rampart) having to be levelled.

The western end of the ditch rested on the Ver across the river from St Michael's village. (There was a footbridge across the river there in the fifteenth century, but horses and wagons would have had to use a ford.) The ditch then followed the lie of the land round modern Kingsbury north-eastwards towards St Peter's. There is no evidence left of the ditch across the northern end of

Remains of Tonman Ditch at Keyfield. *Mike Elliott*

The junction of Marlborough Road and Victoria Street, the site of one of the Bars. Victoria Street was then known as Shropshire Lane. *Mike Elliott*

the town until the site of the former bus garage north of Grange Street. Excavations took place there when the site was developed for housing in the 1990s and did reveal traces of it. The ditch then ran round St Peter's churchyard and on south to Cock Lane.

There is no trace left of how the ditch was finished off south of Sopwell Lane, because the Duke of Marlborough remodelled all of the landscape there for a vast formal garden. It seems, though, that it ran westwards south of Sopwell Lane to join Holywell Hill. This is a blank in the understanding of the medieval defences, because from accounts of fighting in the 1140s it is known that the bridge at the bottom of Holywell Hill was a defended part of the town boundary. Also, whatever features were on the ground in Holywell Hill and between Sopwell Lane and the Ver, they deterred the Yorkists from marching round the ditch and straight on to Holywell Hill.

Bars with moveable 'barriers' (i.e. tree trunks) controlled entry to the main part of the town across the ditch. The main function of the ditch and of these Bars was to stop hostile horsemen being able to ride unobstructed into the town centre. Buildings came right up to the ditch along the roads that crossed it, but for the most part what lay on its townward side were yards, gardens and orchards. These were known as 'the backs' or 'backsides' and Warwick would exploit them in 1455.

It seems unlikely that any part of this system would have had masonry walls, although some of the place names associated with the Bars through the ditch have been used to denote stone defences elsewhere in the country at the time. Several of the chronicles refer to the town as being 'well defended', 'armed' and 'barred and gated'. The Bars (if closed) and the ditches did present an impossible obstacle for horsemen even as a passive defence. If Somerset was leading a largely cavalry force round the outside of the town in the late morning of 17 February 1461, then he could never have surmounted a high bank (up to 33 feet) and was therefore forced to follow the road round to St Peter's.

A last thought on the defences is that they may have been erratic and patchy. The Sopwell Lane Bar held a determined Yorkist attack in the first battle, while the three Bars to the west and north that the Lancastrians had to cross in the second are not even mentioned. One section of the ditch gave Warwick's men no trouble at all in the first battle, while the Lancastrians made no attempt to cross other parts of the ditch in the second. At best the ditch delayed or deflected attacks, but it never stopped a single one in either battle.

Salisbury Hall, owned by Montagu at the time of the second battle (then a moated farmstead). *Mike Elliott*

St Albans is built on a hill, but the topography within the town had no influence on the course of the battles. The Abbey is sited commandingly on the edge of this hill (but not the top), overlooking the river. This siting is very clear when St Albans is seen from a distance, and the most striking view today is from the M25. (The highest point in the town is St Peter's Church.) The Tonman Ditch was built just as the rise of the hill started whenever it could take that advantage of the terrain, and this is best appreciated looking eastwards down Victoria Street from just west of the junction with Marlborough/Upper Marlborough Road. Much of the ditch had to be on level ground, however, and this included the area round Keyfield, where the only serious assault on the ditch against determined defenders took place.

It is likely that a very large number of the combatants in both battles had visited the shrine and the town and were familiar with the local geography. They might also have known that St Albans was a well-supplied town able to accommodate and victual an army and offering opportunities for looting. In addition to that, the Nevilles owned several estates in Hertfordshire. The nearest was Salisbury Hall on the outskirts of the modern city. This was Lord Montagu's local residence at the time of the second battle. (The site passed, via Nell Gwynne, to its eventual modern use as a military museum dedicated to the story of the Mosquito aircraft.)

The Impact of the Battles on the Town

The second battle in particular accelerated the decline in the fortunes of the Abbey, which was already in financial difficulty by the mid-fifteenth century because of endless lawsuits to protect its rights and because of the costs of entertaining royalty on their ever more frequent visits. The looting after the second battle was a financial blow in its own right. In the longer term, the wars were a real deterrent to pilgrims, and numbers never seem to have recovered.

A special twist, though, was that John Morton, who was Chancellor to Edward of Lancaster in 1461 and present at the second battle, took great exception to the Abbey's Yorkist leanings after the battle. When he became Henry VII's Archbishop of Canterbury after 1486, he used his power to undermine and impoverish the Abbey. Cardinal Wolsey later became the first absentee abbot and he used his power further to diminish the Abbey, stripping its assets and bringing it to a parlous state by the time Henry VIII came to dissolve it in 1539. There were just thirty-eight monks left in the end.

St Albans lost the original reason for its existence less than a century after the two battles. Henry VIII dissolved the monasteries and the pilgrims stopped visiting altogether. The town then ceased to have any national significance or special source of income. Its population suffered from attacks of the plague in the sixteenth century and did not grow. This means that the first map in 1634 shows a very similar townscape to the one the combatants would have found.

The redevelopment of later centuries has been largely additional to the medieval street plan rather than sweeping it away. In particular, two new (coaching) roads were built into the town centre by clearing existing buildings. These were London Road from the south-east in 1796 and Verulam Road from the west in 1825–6. (When London Road was completed, the section of Holywell Hill to its north was renamed Chequer Street.)

The following chapter deals with viewing the battlefields, but it may be noted here that the medieval map of St Albans still makes sense on the ground today. Roads from the time of the battles can still be followed and most of the main landmarks from the time are still present. The biggest differences are that there is only a remnant left of the Abbey complex outside the Abbey building itself and only occasional fragments of the Tonman Ditch survive.

Bernards Heath at the Time of the Battles

Bernards Heath was an area of common land in the Parish and Manor of Sandridge. It extended from Sandpit Lane in the south to Beech Bottom in the north. Its western boundary was formed by Luton Lane (now the unmade-up track along the boundary of the heath, not the nineteenth-century Harpenden Road) and it ran eastwards to the estate later known as the Wick or Marshalswick, which was well to the east of the present railway line. Sandridge Road, then the 'King's Highway', ran north–south through the middle of it on up to Sandridge. The first description of the heath was in 1327 and it was then an area of pasturage and woodland surrounded by a hawthorn hedge (presumably stock-proof).

Its most immediate function, though, was as the route for driving livestock into the town from the north. There is still a wide swathe of common land either side of Sandridge Road (the 'Sandridge Road Wastes') protected for that purpose. This suggests that scrub and woodland would not have come right up to the road at the time of the second battle, but that there would have been open ground along the road where horsemen could have deployed. The references to troops becoming ensnared in thickets may relate to what happened to them after their formations had been broken up and they tried to escape the fighting.

Beech Bottom was probably a little deeper and its banks a little taller than as seen today. The greatest difference, however, is that it was most unlikely to have been wooded. Today's magnificent (mostly beech) trees date from the nineteenth century. A picture of the dyke in the 1860s shows only a very few small trees on it. The hawthorn boundary hedge would have run along the bank on the top of the dyke, making it an ideal defensive position.

Only two roads crossed the dyke in 1461. These were Sandridge Road/King's Highway and Harpenden Road/Luton Lane. If the dyke was to be defended, Warwick would have had to secure these two crossing points. (The two other crossings today, at Valley Road and of an earth ramp halfway along the dyke between Harpenden Road and Valley Road, both date from the nineteenth century. The earth ramp is the back of a Victorian rifle range laid out in the bottom of the dyke.)

There are two informative short descriptions of different parts of the Heath from the nineteenth and early twentieth centuries before any substantial development took place on the battlefield.

In the mid-nineteenth century Mary Carbery described the journey from Childwick Green to St Albans:

> The road to St Albans was winding and lonely; wild roses and traveller's joy twined the hedges, primroses and restharrow grew on the banks, and blackthorn and gorse on Barnard's [sic] Heath, a wild place of mounds and pits [from the post-medieval brick fields], where coachmen and footmen sat up very alert and horses pricked their ears, for footpads and fiery tramps lurked among its furzy brakes.

In 1910 the military historian J. E. Wetherell visited the Heath to see what he made of the military topography. He reported that the Heath 'retains much of its original wilderness. ... The Heath was covered with tall grass, thistles, wild raspberries, and a great variety of sturdy weeds.' Both these descriptions tally with the chroniclers' accounts of the Yorkist fugitives becoming entangled in undergrowth and thickets once their formations had been broken up.

Chapter 9

VISITING MODERN ST ALBANS AND BATTLEFIELD TOURS

MODERN ST ALBANS appears at first glance to be a very different place from what it would have been 550 years ago. Urban development spreads more than a mile to the east and south, and the city centre (St Albans was created a city in 1879) has modern shop fronts and shopping centres (The Maltings and Christopher Place). However, a closer look will show that the medieval street plan is still evident. Indeed some of the medieval streets, which began life as the walkways between the market traders' stalls, survive as narrow alleys. All the major medieval roads are still in existence, the one significant change being that a major new east–west thoroughfare was created between 1796 and 1826 with London Road and Verulam Road. In this chapter we will guide you through a visit to St Albans and follow walking and driving routes that illustrate the battlefields and campaigns.

The visitor will usually arrive in St Albans by train or car. By train, you should go to St Albans City on the line to Bedford. From the main station entrance, turn right, walk over the railway bridge and up Victoria Street into the town centre (about a 10 minute walk). If you come in to the Abbey Station via Watford, turn right outside the station, cross over the river and walk up Holywell Hill (again about 10 minutes). By car, park in any of the town centre car parks. While in St Albans, it is worth visiting the Abbey, St Peter's Church, the Clock Tower, Verulamium Park (the site of the Roman city), St Michael's and the two museums (although only the City Museum in Hatfield Road has exhibits relating to the Middle Ages).

The City

Visiting the city today, you will find medieval buildings still standing (and in fifteenth-century form), such as the Abbey and its gateway, the Clock Tower, the Tudor Tavern at the top of George Street, the Boot public house (in the Market Place), St Michael's and St Peter's churches (the latter heavily remodelled in the nineteenth century), and, further afield in Sandridge, St Leonard's Church and the Rose and Crown public house (not called by that name until the sixteenth century).

113

The still imposing Abbey Gateway affords a glimpse of the scale of the Abbey complex in the fifteenth century. *Mike Elliott*

It is worth mentioning here that the half-timbered building currently occupied by W. H. Smith has a plaque on the wall (in Upper Dagnall Street) which claims it is the Moot Hall. Recent research by the St Albans and Hertfordshire Architectural and Archaeological Society has established that this is inaccurate and that the Moot Hall actually stood on the site of the old courtroom located on the ground floor of the Old Town Hall.

NEAR THIS SITE STOOD
THE ELEANOR CROSS
WHERE THE BODY OF
QUEEN ELEANOR
RESTED ONE NIGHT ON ITS
PROGRESS FROM
HARBY TO WESTMINSTER
13 DECEMBER 1290.

The Eleanor Cross in the Market Place disintegrated in the seventeenth century but some pieces of it are said to have been incorporated in a fountain in the old prison (now an office block) near the station. Its position in the Market Place is still marked.

The marker for the Eleanor Cross that stood alongside the Clock Tower. *Mike Elliott*

Fishpool Street, Trollope's line of attack, showing the medieval buildings.
Mike Elliott

There are any number of smaller buildings of the period in St Michael's, Fishpool Street, central St Albans and Sandridge. There are also several buildings in central St Albans, especially in Holywell Hill, which are original to the period but have had new facades since.

We can locate all the Bars. Many are shown on the Hare map and most were also described in the Court of Augmentations' survey of the town under Mary Tudor. Nothing, however, remains on the ground of any of them.

What to see in the Abbey

From the town centre you can find your way to the Abbey through Waxhouse Gate (on the south side of High Street). Waxhouse Gate was an imposing fortification at the time of the battles but is now just a 'gezunder' – the local dialect name for an alleyway that 'goes under' a building.

The Abbey is entered on its south side via the door opposite the modern Chapter House. All the internal embellishments from the period have disappeared except for a Tudor Rose motif ceiling.

From the bookshop (in the South Transept), turn right and proceed to the shrine of St Alban. Now beautifully restored, the shrine is the *raison d'être* for the Abbey, with the wooden medieval watching gallery to the north. In the floor on the south side of the shrine is a memorial to Humphrey, Duke of Gloucester, and his tomb can be viewed through the grating. The twenty-seven tombs and their memorials listed by Ashdown as being in the Abbey are all lost.

The Lady Chapel extends east of the shrine. It was restored in the nineteenth century and now has a black and white tiled floor. Sadly, any evidence of the lords reputedly buried there after the first battle has not survived.

What to see in St Peter's Church

The three tombs listed by Weever in St Peter's Church have been lost during successive repairs and remodellings of the church, but the bodies of Babthorpe (father and son) and of Entwhistle are thought still to lie under the nave floor.

St Peter's Church as it is today. *Mike Elliott*

The Clock Tower

The Clock Tower is open at weekends and Bank Holidays from Easter to the end of September. For a small fee, visitors may climb the ninety-three narrow steps to the top. From here there are excellent views across the city. In particular, the wide sweep of St Peter's Street north to St Peter's Church can be clearly seen. At the time of the battles there would have been only a few low-rise buildings to its north, so look-outs posted there would have had an unimpeded view to the north along the length of St Peter's Street.

It is sobering to imagine the street filled with men in armour engaged in close combat. The 'clokkehouse' was built at the beginning of the fifteenth century and the bell, named Gabriel, was rung during the First Battle of St Albans as a call to arms for the Lancastrian troops in the town centre. You can still hear it ring today as it chimes the hours for the nineteenth-century clock.

Verulamium Park

It is instructive to take in the medieval topography of St Albans before walking the streets. The ideal place to do this is from the top of the Roman wall in the south-west corner of Verulamium Park. There is a generous lay-by with parking here on King Harry Lane. The wall is immediately obvious as a bank running east–west just inside the park.

From the top of this bank the first landmark to be seen is the Abbey itself almost exactly to the north-east. Behind the Abbey and slightly to the left can be seen the brick tower of St Peter's Church on the horizon (it is the only brick church tower other than the Abbey's). This then provides the line of St Peter's Street. To the north-north-east, in the valley at the east and bottom of the park, is St Michael's Church (hidden by trees in the summer). From St Michael's the line of the River Ver can be made out, forming the northern boundary of the park and running on below the Abbey. Fishpool Street runs to its north parallel to the river behind houses. Folly Lane and Catherine Street can be made out by running a line from St Michael's to St Peter's. (Also from St Michael's there is a deliberate straight line of trees running across the park to mark the original route of Watling Street through the Roman city centre.) Lastly, St Stephen's church is out of sight but lies exactly along the line of the Roman wall as it runs off to the east.

Walking Tour 1:
The First Battle of St Albans

Time: You should allow 60–90 minutes to complete this walk. See Map 8.

1. *This walk starts outside the Old Town Hall. From here, proceed northwards through the Town Square (St Peter's Street).*
It was near the site of the present Boots that the Lancastrians raised the Royal Standard. The Moot Hall stood where the Old Town Hall is now and was the headquarters of the royal army.

2. *Turn right at the Cock Inn into Hatfield Road (in the Middle Ages this was known as Cock Lane). After a short distance turn right again into Upper Marlborough Road.*
We are now following the line of the Tonman Ditch. A short way down Upper Marlborough Road on the right stands a post that looks a bit like an old lamp-post but with no lamp. In fact this is a Victorian ventilation pipe from the sewer under the road – the sewer is in the bottom of the ditch and the roadway marks its course at ground level here. With modern development there is nothing of the detail of the ditch itself to be seen, but in places (for example, in Upper Marlborough Road, about 50 yards beyond the

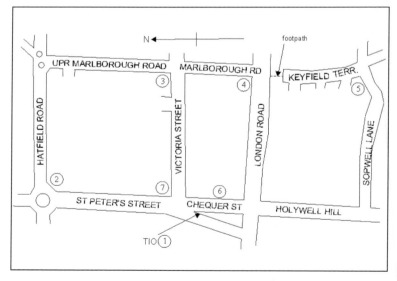

Map 8. Walking Tour 1: First Battle of St Albans (not to scale).

The Old Town Hall. The Tourist Information Office is now in the rear of the building. The Moot Hall stood at the back of this little complex. *Mike Elliott*

The Cock on the corner of Hatfield Road and St Peter's Street. In the Middle Ages this part of Hatfield Road was known as Cock Lane. *Mike Elliott*

Upper Marlborough Road. This modern road follows the line of the Tonman Ditch – which still exists as the sewer. The post on the extreme right is a Victorian sewer ventilation shaft. *Mike Elliott*

junction with Bricket Road) you will notice that the ground on your right is very noticeably higher than on your left, all that is left of the bank that was thrown up when the ditch was dug. The manhole covers mark the line of the ditch.

3. *Proceed down Upper Marlborough Road to the junction with Victoria Street.*
This was the site of the Bar where some of the fiercest fighting occurred. Victoria Street was then known as Shropshire Lane. It was here that the Duke of York made his initial attack. The name 'Tonman' is still commemorated near here in 'Tonman House' (a modern block of Health Authority offices) 50 yards to the east of the junction down Victoria Street.

4. *Cross the road carefully and proceed down Marlborough Road to the junction with London Road.*
It was near this spot that the Earl of Warwick made his decisive attack with the Yorkist reserve.

5. *Cross the road carefully and proceed past the Beehive public house and straight on down Keyfield Terrace until you reach the junction with Sopwell Lane.*

120

The remains of the Tonman Ditch – bank in Upper Marlborough Road. *Mike Elliott*

Pause at Keyfield to take in two features. Looking west across a series of car parks there is clear view to the backs of the buildings on Holywell Hill. This view still illustrates the pattern of the land-holdings at the time of the battle, with long thin plots used as gardens and orchards running from Holywell Hill to the Tonman Ditch. In 1455 the Tonman Ditch would have been tall enough to obscure the view to the back of Holywell Hill, but this relatively open townscape is what Warwick and his men would have seen once they had climbed the rampart. The second feature is the earthen banks you will see opposite the White Hart Tap public house. These are the best surviving remains of the ditch itself.

Keyfield must be one of England's least celebrated historical sites. Nothing here commemorates the fact that it was on this very spot that the Wars of the Roses actually started. In the assembly ground in front of the ditch – now a car park – soldiers buckled their armour and strung their bows before that very first order was given in the wars to advance and engage the king's forces in combat.

Now a quiet side road, in the Middle Ages Sopwell Lane was the main thoroughfare into the town from the east, connecting St Albans to London via Barnet. It was here that the Earl of Salisbury attacked the Bar held by Lord Clifford's men.

London Road and Marlborough Road. Warwick's attack began near here.
Mike Elliott

Turn right and proceed up Sopwell Lane.
We are following the route taken by Salisbury's men as they advanced into the town after being initially held at the Bar.

6. *At the junction of Holywell Hill turn right again. Proceed up Holywell Hill, cross over London Road at the Peahen Hotel and up Chequer Street.*
Note the Cross Keys public house on your right. It was near here that the Earl of Warwick's men broke into the centre of the town. (See below for a detailed discussion of the exact location that Warwick broke through.)

7. *Return to the Town Square.*
Here the battle reached its climax. Across the road from the Old Town Hall, on the corner of Victoria Street, is the site of the Castle Inn. A building society branch now stands there, but an unofficial plaque on the wall (just down Victoria Street) marks where the Duke of Somerset was killed.

122

Sopwell Lane, location of the Bar attacked by Salisbury. *Mike Elliott*

Where did Warwick break through?
The Location of 'Battlefield House'

The critical moment in the first battle is when Warwick, perceiving that the Yorkists are being held at the Bars, finds a way through the town's 'back sides' and breaks through into the town centre, with his men yelling his battle cry: 'A Warwick! A Warwick!' Here (as a result of original research for this work) we attempt to identify as closely as possible the place where this happened.

The relevant passage from the Stow Relation reads:

> The earl of Warwick knowing thereof took and gathered his men together with him and broke in by the garden side into the town between the Sign of the Key and the Chequer in Holywell Street. And as soon as they were within the town they blew trumpets and cried with a loud voice 'A Warwick! A Warwick!', that marvellous it was to hear.

This identifies the breakthrough point as between two inns, the Key and the Chequer. The Key (also known as the Cross Keys) is an interesting one. Over the centuries it has occupied three different locations on Chequer Street. The first inn of that name stood where the London Road now joins Chequer Street and Holywell Hill. This was demolished when the 'new' London Road was driven through in 1796. The public house was re-established on the corner of London Road and Chequer Street. Here it remained until the early twentieth century when it moved again to its present location in the next building up the hill.

The other inn, the Chequer or Chequers (from which Chequer Street derived its name in 1796) no longer exists. According to Ashdown, by the beginning of the twentieth century, the Chequers had become the Queen's Hotel. In an article by Howard Green in *Military Modelling*, there is a photograph showing the Queen's Hotel with a shoe repair shop to the left of the archway. At the time of writing the shoe repair shop is still there, but the hotel is now the Cheltenham & Gloucester building society.

Thus we have defined the limits of the breakthrough site, from the Key in the south (where London Road is now) to the Chequer in the north (the Cheltenham & Gloucester building society). Between these two points are four buildings: a furniture shop on the corner of London Road, the present Cross Keys public house, and two further shops.

Haigh in his account of the first battle says that Warwick 'broke

The Queen's Hotel – as it is now. *Mike Elliott*

The 1907 Pageant procession. Battlefield House is the half-timbered building next to the Cross Keys. *With permission of St Albans Museums.*

through into the market place at what is now called Battlefield House'. This is presumably a reference to Ashdown, who states, 'By the partial demolition of one of the houses, reputed to be "Battlefield House", now occupied by a clothier and an outfitter, the force under Warwick was enabled to break through.' Burne also mentions Warwick's men hacking 'through the walls of what is now known as Battlefield House'. The exact location of Battlefield House is, therefore, intriguing. The authors found a reference on the Internet that described it as an Elizabethan half-timbered building. This makes sense if it was rebuilt after the first battle to replace the buildings damaged by Warwick's attack. Indeed, the name implies an association with the battle. The question remained, where exactly was this building? The answer was finally found in a photograph of the St Albans Pageant of 1907. This shows a view looking up Chequer Street in which a striking half-timbered building can be seen on the right-hand side, just up the hill from the Cross Keys public house on the corner of London Road (as it was then). By comparison with the current scene, it can be deduced that Battlefield House stood on the site of the present Cross Keys.

To summarize, since we can reliably identify the two inns referred to in the Stow Relation, we can safely say that Warwick broke through somewhere in between. The exact place must remain conjectural, although it is almost certainly close to the location of the modern Cross Keys. It is an attractive, if slightly romantic, notion that one might be able to stand in the Cross Keys and imagine Warwick and his men charging through the bar!

After the Battle

Once the fighting was over, the Yorkists were left in control of the town. The dead were removed for burial and the wounded were cared for. An optional addition to the walking tour is to visit first the Lady Chapel in the Abbey, where most of the fallen nobles were taken, and then St Peter's churchyard, where local legend has it that the common soldiers were interred (see Chapter 10).

Walking Tour 2:
The Second Battle of St Albans

Time: You should allow at least two hours to complete this walk. See Map 9.

1. *This walk also begins outside the Old Town Hall. Turn left and walk down French Row to the small road called 'Market Place' with its distinctive medieval clock tower at the end.*
There are several medieval buildings here and it is worth spending a few minutes exploring the area. It was below the Clock Tower that the serious fighting in the battle began. The Lancastrian vanguard had advanced up Fishpool Street, Romeland Hill and George Street only to be repulsed by the Yorkist archers barricaded in the buildings around the square and driven back in confusion. We will now follow the path of the retreating Lancastrians.

2. *Proceed down George Street, Romeland Hill and Fishpool Street until you reach the bridge over the River Ver.*
In the Middle Ages this was the western edge of the town, according to the well-described 1327 boundary. It was here that the Lancastrian vanguard crossed the river and advanced into the town at dawn on the 17th, only to be initially repulsed in the Market Place. As more Lancastrians arrived, further attacks were

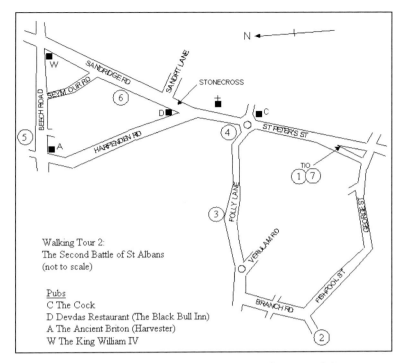

Map 9. Walking Tour 2: Second Battle of St Albans (not to scale).

made up Romeland Hill. Just across the bridge near the entrance to the park is an information panel that mentions the battle.

3. *Walk down Branch Road and, carefully crossing the busy A5183, walk up Folly Lane.*

As the pressure was maintained along the initial line of attack, steadily more elements of the Lancastrian army would have been reaching St Michael's from Watling Street until there were enough to form a second column that attempted to find an alternative point to break in. Following the path of this second column, we now walk round to the north of where the Tonman Ditch used to run. In 1461 this would have been a significant feature, up to 33 feet high in places, and confining the Lancastrians to the road. The Victorian development of what is now called Kingsbury, a hospital, and Victoria Park (on your right) have completely remodelled this landscape since then.

4. *Continue up Folly Lane and Catherine Street.*

The Lancastrians crossed an apparently undefended Bar to come into the town and then debouched into St Peter's Street and broke into the north end of the town. They swung right and attacked the Yorkist archers from the rear. Note that St Peter's Church would have been the northern end of the town in the Middle Ages. The stories surrounding the burial of bodies from both battles at St Peter's are told elsewhere, but the most colourful (and unlikely) is that either because of lack of space, or because of the difficulty in digging frozen ground, many are said to have been buried standing upright and in full armour.

5. *Turn left and, keeping St Peter's Church and then the Devdas Indian Restaurant on your right, proceed down Harpenden Road for about one mile until you reach the Ancient Briton junction with Beech Road.*

The first stretch of road here used to be called 'Bowgate' and just north of St Peter's stood Hall Place (still commemorated as a postal address). Henry VI is alleged to have stayed in Hall Place on the night before the second battle and his sad ghost was said to have appeared out of the panelling on occasion (but see further discussion on Hall Place below). The Devdas Indian Restaurant was the Black Bull Inn in 1461 and then became the Cricketers public house from 1896 to 2005. Harpenden Road was made in the nineteenth century; the road in 1461 was Luton Lane and ran parallel a little to the west. It is now an unmade-up track rejoining Harpenden Road at the Ancient Briton junction.

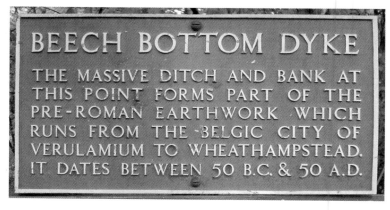

Beech Bottom Dyke. This English Heritage signboard stops at the Roman invasion. *Mike Elliott*

As you walk down Harpenden Road, notice Edmund Beaufort Drive on the left.

The Ancient Briton junction marks the point where the left wing of the Yorkist army was initially deployed to cover the road from the north. Cross over Beech Road and opposite the public house it is possible to view the ancient earthworks of Beech Bottom from just beyond the English Heritage green signboard. These earthworks are 1,500 years older than the Wars of the Roses, but even after 2,000 years they are still formidable, and it is easy to see why the Yorkists incorporated them into their defences. By the early afternoon of 17 February the Yorkists realized that they had been outflanked and their left wing had to be hurriedly redeployed across Bernards Heath to the south-east.

Walk a short distance down Beech Road and turn right into Seymour Road.

This area is now built up but was open heath and scrub at the time of the battle.

6. *When you reach the junction with Sandridge Road, turn right and walk a short distance until you reach the playing field.*

It was on this spot that the battle reached a climax. Montagu's division tried to hold this position, but after fierce fighting were eventually driven back across the heath and defeated. There is an

Bernards Heath looking back towards the site of the town gallows. There is a possible lost burial site in their vicinity. *Mike Elliott*

information panel on Sandridge Road in the middle of the open space that mentions the battle. It was north along Sandridge Road that Warwick made his fighting retreat in the late afternoon of 17 February, harassed by Lancastrian horse.

7. *Proceed back down Sandridge Road to the centre of St Albans.* As you return down Sandridge Road there are two features to note. The first is the avenue of cherry trees. They are alternate red and white trees commemorating the battle for half a mile. Sadly, most of the mature red trees are now dying off, and it is a rare year when the two sets of trees blossom together. The second feature is the very wide verge. This grassland is actually called the 'Sandridge Road Wastes' and is legally protected common land, denoting the traditional use of the road for driving livestock to market in St Albans. This open space around the road may be a significant feature of the ground over which the battle was fought.

Henry VI and Hall Place

In some modern accounts of the first battle it is claimed that Henry VI spent the night before the battle at 'Hall Place', a large house just to the north of the town centre. This building is no longer extant, but there is a small plaque near where it stood explaining this connection between Hall Place and Henry. This is at odds with other accounts (including the Stow Relation), which state that Henry stayed at Watford on the night before the battle.

The Vale Variant of the Stow Relation says, 'The king then being in the place of Edmond Westby, hundreder of the town of Saint Albans.' This is usually taken to refer to Hall Place. Recent research by Gerard McSweeney, however, has shown that this is unlikely. According to the Stow Relation, the king raised his banner 'at the place called Goselowe in Saint Peter street, which place previously was called Sandeforthe'. This is understood to be at or near the junction of Shropshire Lane and St Peter's Street. McSweeney argues that the house of Edmund Westby in which the king resided was not Hall Place but was in the town centre. This fits well with the location of the king's banner (i.e. his head-quarters). It also suggests that Hall Place would have been almost inaccessible to Henry.

There is another local legend (see below) that Henry was lodged in Hall Place prior to the second battle. This is plausible if uncorroborated and would have been a more suitable night-time lodging for a king in winter than the tent he had to occupy during the day.

The site of Hall Place from the west side of St Peter's Street. In the foreground is the site of Bowgate and where the Tonman Ditch crossed the road. *Mike Elliott*

Driving Tour:
The Second Battle of St Albans

This driving tour takes in the whole scope of the second battle from St Michael's to Nomansland. See Map 10.

1. *Take Branch Road out of St Michael's to Verulam Road and turn right towards the roundabout by the petrol station.*
2. *At the roundabout turn left up Folly Lane and on into Catherine Street.*

These two roads do not quite follow the medieval streets – Catherine Street comes out just south of St Peter's Church (while the medieval St Catherine's Lane came out more opposite to it).

This is the point where the Lancastrians had outflanked Warwick's archers in the town centre, split his army and started to defeat it in detail. The chronicles talk of fierce fighting at St Peter's with the Lancastrians driving the main Yorkist force north.

3. *At the roundabout here turn left up St Peter's Street as far as the road junction outside the Devdas Indian Restaurant.*

131

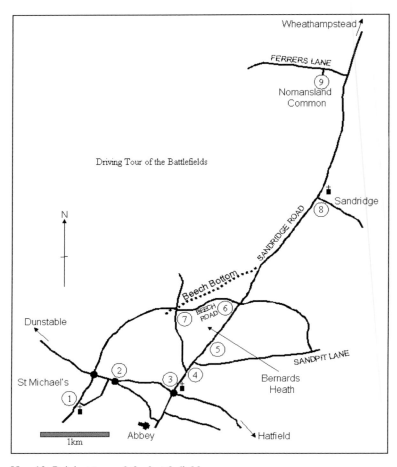

Map 10. Driving tour of the battlefields.

This road used to be called Bowgate. The Devdas Restaurant was the Black Bull Inn at the time of the battle and the Cricketers public house from 1896 to 2005. The left turn is now Harpenden Road but was Luton Lane at the time of the battle.

4. *Take the right turn into Stonecross.*
An actual stone cross was sited in the middle of the junction with Sandpit Lane in the Middle Ages (opposite where the Jolly Sailor public house now stands), marking the northern limit of the town.

5. *Stonecross becomes Sandridge Road after the junction with Sandpit Lane.*

In the Middle Ages the length of this road up to Hitchin via Wheathampstead was known locally as 'The King's Highway'. The open space a quarter of a mile further on is Bernards Heath, where traditionally the Yorkists established a line and held it for some time. The Ordnance Survey map of the battle shows the front line following roughly the modern boundary of the open space and Boundary Road opposite.

See notes in Walking Tour 2 in relation to Sandridge Road (p.130).

The Yorkists were driven off the Heath and into retreat along the King's Highway to Nomansland. The distance from St Michael's to Nomansland is four and a half miles. This makes the battlefield one of the most extended in England. On the day most of the Lancastrians would have had to fight and march this whole distance, but the Yorkists mismanaged their deployment so that their forces came on to the field piecemeal and most would only have had to cover the second two miles.

6. *Turn left at the King William IV public house and drive down Beech Road to the Ancient Briton junction.*

Warwick planned to counter a Lancastrian attack from the north or north-east. The modern Beech Road follows the line of Beech Bottom with the (modern) trees on the dyke clearly visible to the right (north). At the Ancient Briton, Montagu was deployed to cover an attack down Luton Lane. It is worth parking your car near the junction and having a look at the section of Beech Bottom just to the north opposite the public house.

7. *Go back up Beech Road to the King William IV junction.*

Near this spot in 1865 navvies constructing the railway discovered human skeletons and fifteenth-century coins. These were undoubtedly the remains of some of the men killed in the battle, although see the discussion in Chapter 10 about finds relating to the battle here.

Turn left at the traffic lights onto St Albans Road.

This is the old 'King's Highway' and the first stretch is known as Deadwoman's Hill. About a quarter of a mile towards Sandridge the road crosses Beech Bottom. The ditch is almost completely filled in here, but the lines of trees on either side still clearly mark the site. It is tempting to imagine artillery and archers placed on the dyke and on Deadwoman's Hill with arrows being shot downhill able to outrange an enemy approaching on the flat. There is no more likely place on the battlefield for Warwick to have tried to prepare an artillery ambush replicating the French triumph at Castillon.

8. *Proceed now through Sandridge village.*

The village was there at the time of the battle, although the Rose and Crown was so named during the Tudor period. There is no evidence of fighting here, but both armies must have passed through as the Lancastrians pursued the Yorkists northwards. Just north of Sandridge a small country lane diverges off to the right – Coleman Green Lane. This is a remnant of the Roman Stane Street, which ran from Verulamium to Colchester. It would have been the Lancastrians' route had they turned off the Icknield Way onto the Great North Road and then east again at Welwyn. It is likely that the Yorkists would have deployed at least to be aware of an attack from this direction.

9. *Follow the road through Sandridge. A mile further on is Nomansland Common. Turn left into Ferrers Lane and then left again into the car park.*

It is here that some interpretations place the Yorkist vanguard under Norfolk. If, however, the King's Highway was primarily to be defended at the line of Beech Bottom, it seems unlikely that Warwick would have planned to fight a battle here. It is likely, though, that he would have wanted to be aware of any Lancastrian force coming south across the common. Nomansland is where the battle traditionally ends, with the Yorkists rallying for a last stand and the exhausted Lancastrians then withdrawing back to St Albans. The country lane now called Ferrers Lane runs off to the west across the common, and it is most likely that this is the route Warwick took as he retreated that night.

Chapter 10

LIVING HISTORY OF THE BATTLES

IN THIS CHAPTER WE LOOK at how the battles have lived on in oral history and archaeology, in local research and speculation, and in drama and re-enactment. We also seek to answer the most perennial of local speculations – what happened to all the bodies?

Oral History and Legends

Local legends and folk tales are usually coloured and distorted by succeeding generations, and as such should always be treated with great caution by serious historians. This said, oral history does give an indication of the impact that the battles had on the collective memory of the local population and the reports and other stories here show that interest in the battles has lived on in the city and its environs.

There seems to be only one unquestionable example of true oral history relating to either battle. In 1941 Mary Carbery published her memoirs of a Victorian childhood in Childwick Green (pronounced 'Chidwick or Chillick'), a small village a couple of miles to the north of St Albans. (Childwick Green as a village no longer exists and is marked only by a farm and mill on the east side of the River Ver. It is not to be confused with the hamlet now known as Childwickbury).

She reported a conversation, probably held in the early 1880s, which went as follows:

> The cottagers are home keeping and cautious, not caring to venture into towns or go further than to Harpenden fair. They are like this, Bee says, because they believe they are still living in the Middle Ages. The last time a party of them went to St Albans, they found a battle going on and blood flowing in the gutters. The Wars of the Roses were in full swing. They may have seen the body of Henry P., son of Hotspur, lying among the slain that heaped the streets. They saw rough soldiers forcing the weapons of the fallen into the hands of the mild young men of the town and kicking them into the fray.
>
> 'Not our boys, thank 'ee', said the wary women of

Childwick, clutching their sons and scuttling home as fast as they could to the Green, which was hidden by woods and well off the King's Highway [the road to Sandridge and Wheathampstead].

By far the most famous legend associated with either battle is Shakespeare's retelling and acting out of the prophecy that Edmund Beaufort, Duke of Somerset, would die in a castle. The prophecy is recounted in *Henry VI Part 2*, Act 1, Scene IV, where the sorcerer Roger Bolingbroke conjures up spirits who predict that Somerset will die in a castle. The fuller version of the legend (from Halle's and Davies's chronicles, from which Shakespeare drew) has it that he knew of the prediction and took great pains to avoid entering castles. In the play (and in the first battle itself) Somerset takes shelter from the fighting in the Castle Inn. He is killed when he leaves it, demoralized by the realization that he has inadvertently gone into a 'castle'.

Local ghost stories repeated down the centuries can be classed as a type of oral history or legend, and there is a rich vein of them for the battles.

In his study of *Ghosts of the South East*, Tony Ellis includes a section on Battlefield House, St Albans: 'Two separate sounds are heard on the site of Battlefield House. The sound of galloping horses and the clash of steel and shouting of men, remain as a reminder of the two battles fought on the spot.'

There are many other ghost stories associated with the battles that were collected together (in a larger compendium of local hauntings) in the early 1990s by two of the St Albans Honorary Guides. They report:

King Henry VI, who sheltered for a night in Hall Place during the second battle of St Albans in the Wars of the Roses, left his ghost behind in an upper chamber. It drifted in and out of the panelling, before the house was demolished in 1906 [sic]. ...

It seems as if the sounds of some of the hotly contested skirmishes which have taken place in St Albans in past centuries have been imprinted on the sound track of its history.

In his book *Enchanted Britain*, Marc Alexander remarks, 'Battlefield House, built on the scene of the fighting in Chequer Street, St Albans, was known for several hauntings of hoof beats and clashing weapons, which continued after the house was pulled down and replaced with a row of shops.' ...

Aural memories of the Second Battle of St Albans in the Wars of the Roses are said to remain in Folly Lane and Catherine Street, with the occasional sound of quiet footsteps and a muffled drum heard in the early hours, left from the long-ago day when Queen Margaret of Anjou's men crept along this route for a surprise attack on the adversary.

Among the many stories brought to light during the St Albans ghost walks was the following. A lady reported that one night when her daughter and friend were passing St Peter's, very late, the daughter heard the clip-clop of horses' hoofs. As she could see nothing, she thought it was her imagination, but on mentioning it, her friend said she could hear it too. And together they listened as the horses passed, going on towards Bernards Heath.

Archaeology

In general the archaeology of the battles has been disappointing. Urban St Albans has revealed very few military finds and the area of Bernards Heath has been so disturbed by centuries of quarrying for clay that it now has almost no archaeological value.

There are, though, two stories of finds from the second battle, mainly associated with the Midland Railway Company's need for a deep cutting for its main line from Bedford to St Pancras across the north of Bernards Heath in 1866–8.

The first story appeared in the local press in summer 1865, presumably following preliminary clearing and surveying work by the company. It was reported that skeletons and Henry VI coins had been found at 'Deadwoman's Hill near Beech Bottom'. Deadwoman's Hill (etymology unknown) is the sloping stretch of what is now St Albans Road running north to Sandridge from the King William public house to where Beech Bottom intersects the road. The railway does go into a deep cutting here and crosses the still imposing dyke nearby. Local historians Reg Auckland and Chris Reynolds have both drawn attention to this report in the context of the second battle.

The second story is of the finding of a range of other artefacts in the area during the nineteenth century – including cannon balls, a ring, arrowheads, spurs, daggers, a piece of armour, horseshoes, a caltrop and horse brasses – then collected and displayed privately in a local farm. This collection was auctioned off in 1884 and none of the artefacts have ever been seen again. In 1905 there was a local press report of a touring lecture with exhibits (a ring

The nineteenth-century railway embankment meets the Iron Age Beech Bottom Dyke. When the railway was being built there were reports of human remains and other artefacts being found here. *Mike Elliott*

and coins) from the Midland Railway dig but these exhibits too have vanished.

The City Museum is very sceptical about all the artefacts and finds reported from the nineteenth century, and its only exhibit from the area is an undated horseshoe. These finds seem to be where archaeology and local legend shade together, and the lack of evidence today leaves the question of authenticity ever open.

We may be on firmer ground with a story told by John Shrimpton of his father, Robert Shrimpton, who was a distinguished and very long-lived local citizen from the 1520s to the 1620s. He was three times mayor and also left his son a fund of stories about the town and the Abbey before the Dissolution. Robert's account is as follows: 'It seems at [the second battle] they used some cannons or field pieces, for when I was a scholar [at the Abbey School] playing one day … upon the heath without the town, where the fight first began in an old ditch … we found a cannon bullet of iron of a great bigness and weight.'

This find must have been in the mid- to late 1530s and Beech Bottom is the obvious location. The main inference from this find – if it is accepted – is that there was heavy ordnance (and from the

Tower of London) emplaced on the dyke. This would help with an understanding of Warwick's deployments.

The Weather as a local Legend

The supposed weather conditions on 17 February 1461 have led to another local legend. This seems to stem from a comment made by Charles Ashdown that it was snowing on 17 February 1461. Reg Auckland then went on to state that the bodies from the second battle became frozen solid – thus apparently necessitating vertical burial in St Peter's churchyard, which will be explored below.

There are in fact no specific references to the weather in any of the chronicles, so the Meteorological Office was asked for their help. Their records show that the weather in the winter of 1461 was mild over southern England and, in their view, snow and a hard freeze on 17 February would have been most unlikely. Snow (or hail or sleet) on the 17th cannot be completely discounted, but could it be a transpositional error from the Battle of Towton six weeks later, for which there is contemporary evidence?

Exploration, Drama and Re-enactment

The battles are part of living local history in terms of local study, drama and re-enactment. Both the Battlefields Trust and the St Albans Honorary Guides regularly lead walks to explore the two battlefields, thus ensuring that the memory and knowledge of the events as they can be traced on the ground today are not lost.

Both battles have been turned into stage dramas – the first more famously than the second. Shakespeare set Scenes II, III and IV of Act 5 of *Henry VI Part 2* on the battlefield in St Albans town centre on 22 May 1455. This play has been performed ever since it was written and has also been made into film and television.

Shakespeare was a dramatist first, a propagandist for the Tudor monarchy second, and a historian as a poor third. For him the battle was part of a larger drama about blood feuds and the fifteenth-century monarchy and how they led to the triumph of Henry VII's accession. Minor liberties with the facts were perfectly permissible for him, so Margaret, for example, is portrayed as playing an active part in proceedings in 1455 when in reality she was safely in London.

Shakespeare has to place Margaret of Anjou at the heart of the action driving forward events on the day of the battle. The climax of the play is a sword fight between York and Somerset set outside

139

the Castle Inn, with York himself killing Somerset. (This fight never took place, although Somerset was killed outside the inn.) The reasons for this script are obvious. The two protagonists meeting in single combat with swords is excellent drama, and a death in a sword fight is easy to portray on stage.

The second battle enjoyed pride of place in the 1953 St Albans city pageant, 'The Masque of the Queens', on 22–23 June. This pageant celebrated Elizabeth II's coronation by depicting great scenes in local history when various queens had visited the city. It was written by Cyril Swinson, who consulted original sources with help from the City Librarian. It stands as an interpretation of the battle in its own right.

Margaret has to take centre stage again for dramatic reasons to honour the theme of the pageant. Margaret does not herself lead the Lancastrians in battle, but is in the forefront of the action. The masque opens with Warwick congratulating himself on the thoroughness of his defences while Margaret advises her commanders on how to circumvent them. Events are then compressed in time and space for dramatic effect to a short period and around St Peter's Church, including the executions of prisoners after the battle. The play ends with Margaret preparing to direct the victorious Lancastrians to advance against the other Yorkist army in the west.

This is the only interpretation that makes the intention to fight the two Yorkist armies separately the key element of Lancastrian strategy. For the wider picture, though, the masque follows Shakespeare's interpretation of the Wars of the Roses.

There have been any number of re-enactments of the battles over the last

An archer from the 1907 Pageant. *With permission of St Albans Museums.*

140

century. These have ranged from small-scale meticulously researched events, such as the 550th commemoration of the first battle in May 2005, through to large-scale civic mêlées in fancy dress, such as at the 1907 city pageant. Looking at the pictures of the several pageant re-enactments from 1907 to 1953, it is obvious that fun rather than authenticity was the keynote.

Where are the Monuments and Bodies?

By the end of 1461 there were dozens of memorials and thousands of graves from the two battles, but it is easier for the modern visitor to be taken to the site of an alleged haunting than to an authenticated burial. The story and the speculation about how the exact location of all the bodies, especially those from the second battle, came to be lost to posterity is a mixture of antiquarianism, myth and archaeology.

There is no mystery, first, about most of the more famous of the fallen after the first battle being taken to the Abbey's Lady Chapel and interred there with memorials. There is, however, nothing to be seen of them at all today, because they were deliberately destroyed during the Reformation and no attempt seems to have been made to preserve any vestige or memory of them *in situ*. John Weever, who carried out a comprehensive survey of English funeral monuments published in 1631, visited the Abbey (by then just the parish church for the central area of St Albans). His report was that the 'funeral trophies are wasted with devouring time, and seats or pews for the townsmen made over their honourable remains'. Some people did remember still that the Lady Chapel once housed the bodies of Somerset, Clifford and Northumberland. John Shrimpton, as mentioned earlier, added that all the fallen nobles had been given brasses on the floor, but that these had been taken up to make it easier to set out the pews Weever refers to.

Worse was to follow. The Lady Chapel became a school, and a public road was built through the Abbey across the chapel's western end. What the Reformation had started generations of schoolboys completed in terms of defacing the fabric of the building. The church was promoted to a cathedral in 1877, but not before it had seriously started to collapse. A massive restoration programme was undertaken from 1864 onwards. This work led to the rediscovery of the whole of the shrine to St Alban, which had been used as road fill. There were also stories of skeletons being found in the excavations under the Lady Chapel. There was, though, no way of knowing whose bones they were, so their graves and identities remain lost to this day.

Brass of Henry Bourchier, Earl of Essex from Little Easton Church, Essex. This is one of the very few tombs and monuments of any of the combatants to have survived. *By kind permission of Little Easton Parish Church.* *Photograph: Peter Burley*

The most persistent local story about the bodies of the common people from both battles is that they were buried in a mass grave (or graves) in St Peter's churchyard. This is sometimes embellished by the account of the bodies being buried in a trench, standing up, still in full armour and being frozen solid because of the weather (in February 1461). Local historian Charles Ashdown talked to the sexton at St Peter's (in an account published in 1893), who told him that he was always turning up bits and pieces on the north side of the graveyard that he attributed to the burials after the battles.

The story of the strange mass grave is often repeated in St Albans and has been retold by local historians and travel writers. The story with all its embellishments is inherently implausible and bears no relation to known medieval military or ecclesiastical burial practices. It also has no archaeological credentials. It does, though, merit careful investigation, because there is no memorial to the fallen and it is right that we should try to establish where they were.

The authors' correspondence with the church confirms their belief that there are burials from the battles associated with it.

There is, however, definitely no mass grave within the current curtilage of the graveyard, which has been thoroughly and properly investigated. (The graveyard is now managed as a local park and has free access at all times.)

There is a tale, meant to support the idea of the burials at St Peter's, of artefacts relating to the second battle being displayed there in the nineteenth century. The eminent historian Sir James H. Ramsay wrote in 1895: 'Another man executed [after the second battle] was William Gower, who had carried one of the king's banners in the action. In the vestry of St Peter's Church may be seen a helmet, a relic of the battle: also a pair of fetters found on the leg bones of a man of great stature – perhaps Kyrielle [sic], Bonville, or Gower.' Local archaeologists Rosalind Niblett and Isobel Thompson are able to shed some light on this story. The helmet was a decoration from a sixteenth-century tomb and is now in the museum. (The 'fetters' may have enjoyed the same provenance.)

The story of the mass grave or graves can in fact be traced back to John Weever again, but he also strips it of its embellishments. Weever wrote as though he had visited St Peter's and said, 'This Church and Churchyard was stuffed full with the bodies of such as were slain in the two battles, fought here at St Albans.'

He goes on to list the known memorials to Entwhistle, Packington and the Babthorpes in the church, but adds that by his day most of the memorials had been defaced. These have subsequently disappeared completely. Weever's turn of phrase suggests that every spare plot and space was turned over to disposing of the bodies, rather than there being one mass grave. There is a further possibility at St Peter's that might reconcile some of the various elements of the local folklore – the possibility that the bodies were initially stacked in the Tonman Ditch, which then ran round the churchyard, while the graves were being dug – but this is pure speculation.

Rosalind Niblett and Isobel Thompson investigated the sources and archaeology relating to the stories about the bodies in their 2005 study of the city for English Heritage. They point out that in the fifteenth century there was an arrangement for St Peter's to be used for town burials, which would otherwise have been in the Abbey precincts at the Abbey Parish's church – St Andrew's Chapel. They have also catalogued a number of reported finds of bones over the centuries, when foundations were being dug in ground north and south of the present churchyard. Not all of these can be confirmed as human and none were properly recorded. Their tentative conclusion, however, is that the medieval graveyard may have been larger than the current one and that there is scope for at least some of the bodies from the battles being interred in that larger area.

There is, though, another account, potentially from within living memory, of the battles, from John Shrimpton. This is that not all the commoners' bodies were interred at St Peter's itself, but that the church used an over-spill burial ground on Bernards Heath for them. No such burial ground has ever been found, but then the land concerned has been the most disturbed and dug-up part of the Heath over the centuries. The part of the Heath nearest to St Peter's also contained the town gallows, so there might have been a tradition of interments there associated with them. The authors feel that this account of an additional, but now completely lost, burial ground managed by St Peter's but outside the town may be the best explanation of what happened to the fallen and reconciles several elements of the stories.

One other story relating to bodies in the town itself comes from a Victorian find of bones at the site of the Sopwell Lane Bar. This was taken at the time to prove the ferocity of the fighting there in the first battle. Niblett and Thompson, however, dismiss the possibility of a couple of stray bodies being overlooked and left *in situ* and, of course, there is no proof that the bones were human.

There is a local story further afield about the slain from the northern part of the 1461 battlefield. (This would be the area where the Yorkists had broken ranks and were being ridden down by Lancastrian horsemen.) Reg Auckland went on to speculate from the 1865 Midland Railway finds that the railway embankment, where the track intersects Beech Bottom, now covers a mass grave. This has to remain a plausible suggestion, but unconfirmed. There was, however, no follow-up to the 1865 finds, the authorities seem to have paid the skeletons no attention, and the corroborating coins have vanished for over a century. That said, the spot itself is accessible today (from open space in the Valley Road housing estate) and is an awesome and thought-provoking place.

Chapter 11

WEAPONS, ARMOUR AND ARMIES OF THE WARS

T HIS CHAPTER COVERS the composition of the armies that fought in the Wars of the Roses, how they were raised, their equipment, and how they deployed for battle.

Raising an Army

The medieval practice of feudalism which began in the late thirteenth century, where a man gained right of tenure in return for military service to his lord, had largely died out by the fifteenth century, having been largely replaced by a process known variously as 'bastard feudalism', 'livery and maintenance' or 'neo-feudalism'. Dr Bothwell describes it as 'a natural successor to the feudal system as it replaced hereditary land tenure with indenture for service for the lifetime of the retained'. Under this arrangement, a lord entered into a contract with a man, in which the lord paid him an annual retainer and fed and clothed him (in his livery) in return for service both in peace and war. The written contract was known as an indenture or letter patent and was valid for a fixed period, often for life. Although Richard II had attempted in 1390 to limit the wide-spread use of livery and maintenance, many lords continued to raise what amounted to private armies.

As noblemen recruited these indentured retainers, groups of men who owed allegiance to a particular lord were formed and these were known as 'affinities'. They were often geographically based, so that a nobleman would recruit retainers from the local gentry. Some of them might be nobility themselves, so that a complex network of allegiances and indentures was created. Indeed, some men could be indentured to more than one lord. This could give rise in some circumstances to doubts as to whom a given man would actually support in a crisis.

The other method of raising troops was the Commission of Array. This can be likened to the regulations concerning the raising of militia forces in later centuries. As Anthony Goodman says: 'Commissions of array were used more specifically to provide for the defence of the realm, as well as for expeditions abroad.'

A particular example of this method was that of Sir John Wenlock just before the Second Battle of St Albans. Goodman notes, 'In January 1461, when preparations were being made to resist the queen's advance on London, Sir John Wenlock had his commission to suppress her sympathizers strengthened by the power to call together the lieges of Hertfordshire and five other shires north of the city.' Most campaigns in the Wars of the Roses were quite short and so there would be little, if any, time for training of the troops raised by Commission of Array. 'Probably masses of hastily arrayed contingents,' writes Goodman, 'often brought into battle within days of assembling, could only be expected to line up for a frontal assault or defence with their traditional weapons, bow and bill.'

Troop Types

There were several types of troops in a Wars of the Roses army. The core of the army was formed of heavily armoured men-at-arms. These were supported by billmen and the ubiquitous archers. There might be a few mounted knights or men-at-arms, but this was often confined to just the leaders. Horses were, however, used on the march by as many as could obtain them. Mobile artillery was just coming into use, enabling it to be used on a battlefield rather than only for siege work. There were also experimental troops armed with handguns, who were usually brought in from the continent. Finally, there were lighter mounted troops used specifically for scouting purposes.

Archers

The bowmen of England and Wales had gained a formidable reputation in the Hundred Years War as the battle-winning arm at the famous battles of Crécy, Poitiers and Agincourt. They were particularly effective when used in combination with dismounted cavalry and infantry.

According to Matthew Strickland, the origins of the longbow can be traced back as far as the Neolithic period, and both Sean McGlynn and Strickland demonstrate the continuous history of the bow from the early Middle Ages. It started to be widely used by the English following Edward I's campaigns in Wales during the late thirteenth century.

The longbow was usually made of yew (although elm could also be used), and was at least as tall as the man who used it. The bow string was made of hemp. The full-length longbow, with a draw weight in excess of 100 pounds had a draw length of between 30 and 36 inches.

An archer learned to shoot from an early age, and when properly trained (after years of practice) would be able to shoot accurately at a range of up to 300 yards. A variety of arrowheads were used, some of which were designed specifically for their armour-penetrating capabilities (see p.38). At close range the longbow was deadly – even to a man in plate armour. Compared to the crossbow, the longbow had a phenomenal rate of fire – a trained archer could draw and loose up to twelve arrows a minute. Sometimes the skies over the battlefield were literally darkened by the arrow storm.

The problem with the longbow was that it took years of practice to master. From Edward I's time onwards it was a legal requirement that on a Sunday, in every English village, the peasants had to practise archery at the butts. The French preferred the crossbow, a much easier weapon to learn to use, which had a similar range and penetrative power as the longbow, but could only shoot a maximum of three or four quarrels in a minute. During the Wars of the Roses both sides used the longbow and as a result it rarely gave either side a clear advantage. At the First Battle of St Albans, however, only the Yorkists had an adequate force of archers and this factor was to prove decisive.

A description of English archers by the Italian scholar Dominic Mancini in 1483 says:

> There is hardly any without a helmet, and none without bows and arrows; their bows and arrows are thicker and longer than those used by other nations, just as their bodies are stronger than other peoples', for they seem to have hands and arms of iron. ... The common soldiery have more comfortable tunics that reach down below the loins and are stuffed with tow or some other soft material. They say the softer the tunics the better do they withstand the blows of arrows and swords, and besides that in summer they are lighter and in winter more serviceable than iron.

Some archers (and presumably other troops) used horses as transport, but not for fighting, as Mancini again says:

> Not that they are accustomed to fight from horseback, but because they use horses to carry them to the scene of the engagement, so as to arrive fresher and not tired by

the fatigue of the journey: therefore they will ride any sort of horse, even pack-horses. On reaching the field of battle the horses are abandoned.

Archers might carry a stake pointed at each end, particularly if they expected to encounter a mounted enemy, but this was rarely the case in our period.

Billmen

The majority of the foot soldiers were equipped with a variety of armour, from a simple padded 'jack' up to full plate armour. Armour was expensive and often foreign-made (particularly in Italy) and consequently was commonly handed down from father to son. Thus a typical army of the period would have men wearing many different types of armour and in various states of completeness.

Their main weapon was the bill, also called a 'brown bill' or 'black bill'. It was a polearm with a wide cutting blade, with or without spikes and hooks in various places, which was derived from the common agricultural billhook. Bills came in a large variety of shapes and sizes. Billmen might alternatively be equipped with other similar polearms, such as the guisarme, a large spear-like polearm, or the glaive, a polearm with a broad

blade and a single cutting edge. The latter was essentially a long knife on the end of a pole. The partisan was similar to the guisarme. It had a broad double-edged blade rather like a sword about two feet long with lugs of various designs at the bottom.

There is a school of thought that contends that there are no contemporary references to 'billmen' as such, and that in fact the term 'men-at-arms' is all-embracing, covering close-fighting troops of all types, from lightly armoured men (with probably just a

Padded 'jack'. *Peter Shepherd*

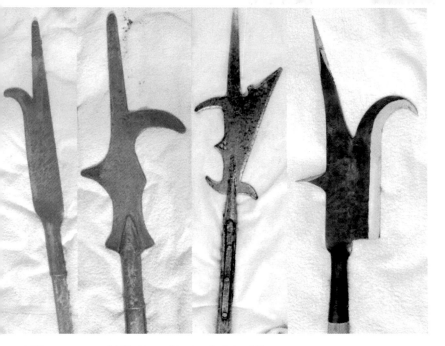

Different types of bill. *Peter Shepherd, John Kliene*

padded 'jack') through to fully equipped men in complete 'white harness'.

In the Bridport Muster Roll of 1457, of the 100 soldiers present, about two-thirds were archers while the rest were equipped with a variety of weapons, including bills, glaives, spears and poleaxes. This suggests that the term 'billman' is not necessarily confined to those troops that carried the English 'brown bill' but also included those armed with other polearms. It seems that local troops such as these mustered with whatever weapons and armour they could lay their hands on.

Mixed retinues were more common in the later fifteenth century than before. For example, in 1452, the 290 men contracted by Walter Strickland for service with the Earl of Salisbury comprised 140 bowmen and 150 billmen.

On balance it is the authors' view that billmen did in fact exist in fifteenth-century armies, albeit that it may have been a some-what generic term and that some 'billmen' may well have been equipped with polearms other than the 'brown bill' and probably had a variety of armour. The term 'men-at-arms' seems to relate specifically to those armoured close-fighting troops in the in-dentured retinues of the lords.

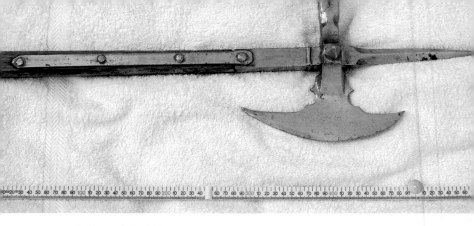

Pollaxe. *John Kliene*

Men-at-arms

The fully equipped man-at-arms, encased in full plate armour and wielding one or more of a variety of vicious close-quarter weapons, formed the core of the army. By the second half of the fifteenth century, the transition from mail to plate was more or less complete. The men-at-arms mostly fought on foot, but occasionally could be mounted, as, for example, in the two Lancastrian cavalry charges at Blore Heath in 1459.

The weapons that could be used by dismounted men-at-arms were many, including various types of swords, maces, war hammers, axes and polearms. The 'pollaxe' in particular was a weapon mostly used by men-at-arms.

The term 'pollaxe' is a bit of a misnomer. First, 'poll' is a medieval word relating to the skull, and has nothing to do with its being a polearm. Secondly, the weapon often did not include an

Glaive. *John Kliene*

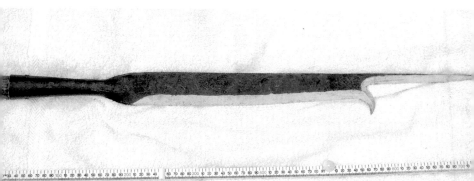

axe blade at all. A more accurate name for the weapon is *hache*, the French word for axe. There were apparently two main types of *hache*. One had an axe-shaped blade with a small hammer or curved spike behind. The other had a hammer head rather than an axe, with a spike or curved fluke to the rear. This latter type was also known as a *Bec de Faucon*. The anonymous fifteenth-century treatise, *Le Jeu de la Hache*, translated into modern English by Dr Sydney Anglo, describes fighting techniques for use with the pollaxe.

Fore-riders

The 'fore-riders', also known as 'scourers' or 'prickers', were lightly equipped mounted scouts. These troops did not fight in the line of battle, as Anthony Goodman explains:

> There was an enhanced need for troops of light horse – '*scourers*' (also termed '*aforeriders*' or '*prickers*') to protect the flanks of footmen and waggons, and maintain contact between columns, as well as watching enemy movements and reconnoitring objectives.

These troops were typically equipped with some armour, such as a 'brigandine' (a leather or heavy fabric coat with many small plates attached to it to give both protection and flexibility) and a 'sallet' helmet, with maybe one or two smaller pieces of plate armour if the individual had such available.

In his account of the Second Battle of St Albans, Gregory makes it clear that he believed that the failure of the 'prickers' to warn the Yorkists of the Lancastrian advance (or Warwick's failure to take

A fore-rider (scourer) in brigandine and sallet. *John Kliene*

151

their news seriously) was one of the main reasons for Warwick's defeat. Gregory himself was a foot soldier and it is amusing to read his highly biased views on the usefulness of the Yorkist cavalry: 'As for spearmen they are only good to ride before the footmen and eat and drink up their victuals, and many more such fine things they do. You must hold me excused for these expressions; for in foot soldiers is all the trust.'

Handgunners

The handgun was still very new at this time and was carried by specially trained men, often mercenaries from Burgundy. It was used, probably for the first time in a pitched battle on English soil, at the Second Battle of St Albans. The handgun was slow and difficult to use, as Gregory relates: 'And before the gunners and Burgundians could level their guns they were busily fighting.'

Due to the length of time it took to load and discharge their weapons, the handgunners needed some form of protection and wore a breastplate, sallet helmet and bevor (a chin and throat defence). They would fight from cover if possible, or if not, use a pavise, a large portable shield with a folding rear support.

Although by the fifteenth century the effectiveness of heavy cannon in siege warfare was clearly understood, it is unlikely that handguns had been used widely in England before and they appear to have attracted a great deal of interest. Handguns had first appeared on the continent in the late fourteenth century. Originally they were in effect miniature cannons, with a short barrel attached to a wooden or iron stock, which was either held against the chest or under the arm. They often had a hook attached underneath so that they could be hooked over a convenient wall or log to absorb the recoil. They were originally fired by a red hot wire or coal. By the time of the Second Battle of St

Albans the first matchlock firearms had begun to appear and it is possible that the Burgundians had brought some of these with them. With the matchlock the stock or butt was held against the shoulder. The match cord was prepared by soaking it in a mixture of saltpetre and horse urine. The gun was fired by a smouldering piece of cord or match, which was held in a clamp known as a serpentine. When the trigger was pulled it caused the serpentine to swivel, plunging the glowing tip of the match into the priming powder in the pan.

Compared to the longbow, these early handguns were inaccurate, unreliable and very slow to reload. It is easy to imagine the scorn and derision with which the archers in Warwick's army would have regarded these new weapons. However, the weapon had one great advantage over the longbow – whereas it took years of training to produce a skilled archer capable of handling a longbow, almost any man could be trained to fire a gun in a few days. During the sixteenth century the longbow gradually disappeared from the battlefield, while the matchlock became the standard infantry weapon, only being replaced during the final decades of the seventeenth century when the more reliable flintlock musket appeared.

Artillery

Guns had been in use for siege warfare since the fourteenth century. By the time of the Wars of the Roses, lighter more mobile pieces were being developed, so that for the first time artillery could be deployed on the battlefield. Ammunition consisted of a variety of stone and metal balls and even large metal arrows. Gregory notes, 'for the Burgundians had such instruments that would shoot both pellets of lead and arrows of an ell in length with six feathers, three in the middle and three at one end, with a very big head of iron at the other end, and wild fire, all together.'

These arrows must have looked very strange! (An ell is a measure of length, about 45 inches.) The lighter pieces were relatively mobile, being mounted on wheeled carriages. Anthony Goodman notes that:

> This company's guns, unlike the single barrel pieces more familiar in England, were *'ribaldekins'* – multiple-barrels designed to fire simultaneously lead pellets, iron-headed arrows and 'wild fire'. They were aimed through the shutters of pavises, part of the gunners' elaborate defences. At St Albans the gunners were probably attacked before they could erect their booby-traps satisfactorily.

On the other hand, Smith and DeVries in their book on the artillery of the Dukes of Burgundy maintain that *rebaudequin* actually referred to the type of carriage on which the guns were mounted.

Armour

The man-at-arms typically wore a full plate armour known as a 'harness' or 'white harness'. The latter term referred to the fact that the armour was plain metal, possibly polished. The finest armours were manufactured in Italy, for example in Milan, or Germany, and in the fifteenth century the development of plate armour reached its peak. The full harness consisted of pieces each designed to fit a particular part of the body, but still allowing the man to move and fight.

The fifteenth-century text 'How a Man Shall be Armyd' describes the procedure for putting on such a full harness. The foundation is an 'arming doublet' fitted with laces (known as 'points'), by which the armour can be attached, a pair of hose on the legs with additional padding to prevent chafing, and finally shoes also fitted with points. The first to be fitted are the sabatons, articulated pieces for the feet. These are followed by the greaves (lower leg) and cuisses (thighs). The poleyns (knee defence) are attached to the cuisses. The tassets are then fitted round the hips, and the breast and backplates are hinged together at one side and buckled on. The arms are protected by the vambraces on the forearms and the rere-braces on the upper arms, with gauntlets for the hands. The elbows are protected by the couters and the shoulders by the pauldrons. Sometimes the armpit has an additional defence called a besagew.

It is interesting that the treatise says that a short sword is held by a ring rather than a scabbard 'that it may be lightly drawn'.

There were several different styles of helmet in use

Bascinet. *John Kliene*

Sallet. *John Kliene*

during the period. The bascinet, a basin-shaped helmet, was originally open-faced, but later a visor was added. Bascinets were used from the mid-fourteenth century, and were still occasionally used in the early sixteenth century. The armet, a close-fitting helmet with a visor and hinged cheek pieces appears to have originated in Italy sometime before 1450 and remained in use until the sixteenth century. The armet was lighter and more protective than the bascinet. The less common barbute or barbuta was a close-fitting helmet that came in a variety of open and close-faced forms and originated in Italy in the mid-fifteenth century. The most popular design had a Y- or T-shaped slot in the face to provide vision and ventilation, and was clearly modelled on ancient classical Greek helmets. The sallet or salade was a basin-shaped helmet often with a small, hinged visor, and a long, articulated tail, to protect the back of the neck. It was in use in the fifteenth and sixteenth centuries.

A soldier who could not afford a better helmet often had a kettle hat – a plain iron hat with a broad brim, similar to some helmets of the twentieth century. The kettle-hat was in common use from the twelfth to the fifteenth centuries.

Organization and Battle Deployment

Commonly an army of the Wars of the Roses was organized in three 'battles', known as the foreward (or vanguard), the main battle and the rearward. Typically, these three battles would form in line when the army deployed, with the vanguard on the right and the rearward on the left. If there was insufficient room, they might form up with two battles in front and one (usually the main battle) in reserve. The main battle was commanded by the senior commander present, the others by his immediate subordinates.

In a given tactical situation, detachments might be formed for specific duties, as, for example, the force of archers who held the town centre against the Lancastrian advances in the Second Battle of St Albans.

Field defences were extensively employed at the Second Battle of St Albans. The use of field defences in the form of fortified artillery encampments had become a standard tactic by the second half of the fifteenth century. What was unusual, in fact unique, about the second battle is the suggestion that Warwick had four miles of linear field defences. The authors believe that Dixon's alternative suggestion, that Warwick intended to have a fortified artillery encampment on Bernards Heath, is perfectly logical and fits in with contemporary accounts.

How did a fifteenth-century English army deploy in the field? We can discount the light mounted troops as mentioned earlier, but we need to consider the tactical deployment of men-at-arms, billmen, archers, handgunners and artillery. First let us look at the relationship between men-at-arms and archers.

Bearing in mind that the development of tactics is always based on those of the previous war, the deployment of the English army at Agincourt (1415) must be taken into consideration here. After all, Agincourt occurred only forty years before the First Battle of St Albans and so could have been remembered by some of the participants – or at least by their fathers. The traditional view is that at Agincourt the English men-at-arms were deployed in three blocks with 'wedges' of archers in between and wings of archers on each flank of the army, angled forward. There is an increasing trend to discount this view. Matthew Bennett has suggested that the meaning of Froissart's *en herce* actually relates to the positioning of the men in successive ranks alternately rather than one behind the other. Thus each man would be like a spike in a harrow. This idea is further developed by Robert Hardy, who uses the term 'quincunx' to describe the archer formations. Hardy continues by suggesting that the archers were formed up not only on the flanks of each body of men-at-arms but also *in front of* them. He then develops this idea further:

> It is worth examining in detail three battles which strongly suggest the use of archers across the battle-front of English armies … [There are] reasons to believe they are exemplars of the 'archers in front' deployment. That it is not often believed in by historians writing today is possibly because we have so little evidence of any drilled manoeuvre among the soldiers of the Middle Ages, and absolutely no written evidence of how such putative movements might have been put into practice, though a little thought may suggest perfectly simple ways in which retiring archers could slip

into alleys left open between men-at-arms or disperse to the wings while still shooting.

Hardy goes on to show that at each of three battles, Bulgnéville (1431), Verneuil (1424) and Formigny (1450), there is evidence to suggest that archers did indeed form up in front of the men-at-arms.

We have discussed this in some depth in an attempt to demonstrate that, far from being devoid of any tactical skill, fifteenth-century commanders had a real understanding of the relative capabilities of their fighting men and used them accordingly. The big difference between the battles of the Hundred Years War and those of the Wars of the Roses is that in the latter *both* sides had archers – the effective tactics of Poitiers, Crécy and Agincourt would no longer be successful. More than one account of battles in the Wars of the Roses talk of an initial archery duel and there is the well-documented case of the Yorkist archers at Towton making use of the poor visibility in order to confuse the opposing Lancastrian archers into firing at too great a range and thus winning the archery contest. There are a few occasions when one side did have superior numbers of archers. For example, at the First Battle of St Albans, the number of recorded arrow wounds suffered by the Lancastrians suggests that the Yorkists had a stronger archer contingent.

So, then, we have established that bodies of archers were frequently deployed in front of the men-at-arms to engage in an initial archery duel and then fall back behind the close fighting troops. What about the billmen? In the discussion on how troops were raised it is evident that retinues that were raised together would, of necessity, fight together under the command of the men responsible for raising them. Since billmen, like men-at-arms, were the close-fighting troops, it is likely that both types were brigaded together (thus compounding the idea that billmen as a specific troop type did not exist). Thus indentured retinues of men-at-arms would take the field supported by bands of billmen raised by commission of array. Whether the billmen formed up on the flanks of the men-at-arms or in rear support cannot be determined: suffice to say that this would probably have varied depending on the tactical situation.

Mounted troops, if used at all, would be deployed on the flanks of the army, as a reserve, or, as at Tewkesbury, in a hidden flank location in order to deliver a surprise attack (assuming that the '200 spears' were in fact, mounted). The forces at the First Battle of St Albans, being deployed to attack or defend the town's defences, were almost certainly on foot, except for one reference to York trying to lead his men mounted until his horse was killed under him.

Handgunners, where available, would be in the front rank of a battle – nobody would want to get between these dangerous weapons and the enemy! Artillery was most likely deployed either in the gaps between battles or in front of a battle if it was intended to fight a defensive engagement. There is growing evidence to suggest that an alternative tactical deployment of artillery was to create a fortified artillery encampment. Such an encampment was successfully used by the French at Castillon in 1453. The Yorkists had tried to employ a similar tactic at Ludlow in 1459, and the Lancastrians at Northampton in 1460. It is possible that this was also Warwick's intention at the Second Battle of St Albans.

There are specific references to the uses of these weapons in the chronicles for the second battle in particular. Warwick's archers are quoted as stopping the first Lancastrian attack. We have seen that Gregory had a lot to say about the handgunners and about the nets, pavises and caltrops used by the Yorkists. At least one caltrop found an intended target when Andrew Trollope stood on it and was immobilized. Several chronicles talk of the advance of Somerset's main body on horseback, and then we have

Men-at-arms from the 1948 Pageant. Re-enactment has come a long way since! *With permission of St Albans Museums. Copyright Photo Precision Ltd., Holywell Hill, St Albans (the company is no longer in business)*

Gregory's explicit reference to the horse being used to ride down and spear fleeing Yorkists. We have noted how the effectiveness of body armour meant that there were almost no casualties among those wearing it. We have also shown how these references can be interpreted against a wider understanding of medieval warfare.

Conclusion

In Shakespeare, the Earl of Warwick delivers the ironic line that the Duke of York's victory in 1455 'Shall be eterniz'd in all age to come'. Ironic because the 'victory' propelled the protagonists into cycles of conflict and often ignominious death.

We have shown why and how these cycles started in St Albans. We have followed them to bring many of the same people, or their children, back in 1461. We have unravelled the problems of this second battle that brought the Wars of the Roses to a cusp. One more Lancastrian effort after their stunning triumph could have ended the wars. It was one effort too far, though, and the cycle turned again to put Edward IV on the throne.

This has also been the Earl of Warwick's story, with triumph at the first battle and humiliation at the second showing the opposite poles of his complex character and capacities.

The town of St Albans was scarred by the battles but then all trace of them was effaced, creating a very different type of 'fog of war', which we have tried to penetrate. The modern city, though, remains one of the best-preserved and most explicit of all the battlefields of the Wars of the Roses, and we would like this to be properly understood and acknowledged.

Lastly, we would like the story of these two battles to be a memorial to the thousands who fell in them because, at the time of writing, they have no other.

Appendix A

MUSEUMS, CHURCHES, CLUBS AND SOCIETIES

Museum of St Albans
Hatfield Road, St Albans, Hertfordshire AL1 3RR
Phone: 01727 819340
Email: history@stalbans.gov.uk

Verulamium Museum
St Michael's Street, St Albans, Hertfordshire AL3 4SW
Phone: 01727 751810
Email: museums@stalbans.gov.uk

National Army Museum
Royal Hospital Road, Chelsea, London SW3 4HT
Phone: 020 7730 0717 (switchboard)
Email: info@national-army-museum.ac.uk

St Peter's Church
St Peter's Street, St Albans, Hertfordshire AL1 3HG
Phone: 01727 855485 (Tuesday–Friday 9.30 a.m.–12.30 p.m.)
Email: mail@stpeterschurch.uk.com
Web: www.stpeterschurch.uk.com

Cathedral and Abbey Church of St Alban
Sumpter Yard, Holywell Hill, St Albans, Hertfordshire AL1 1BY
Phone: 01727 890200; 01727 860780
(Information Desk: Monday–Saturday 10.30 a.m.–4.30 p.m.)
The Dean, The Deanery, Sumpter Yard, St Albans AL1 1BY
Email: dean@stalbanscathedral.org.uk
Web: www.stalbanscathedral.org.uk

The Battlefields Trust
Meadow Cottage, 33 High Green, Brooke, Norwich NR15 1HR
Phone: 01508 558145
Email: national.coordinator@battlefieldstrust.com
Web: www.battlefieldstrust.com

The Battlefields Trust: London & South East
Web: www.btlse.co.uk

The St Albans and Hertfordshire Architectural and Archaeological Society

64 Marshalls Drive, St Albans, Hertfordshire AL1 4RF
Phone: 01727 856250
Web: www.stalbanshistory.org
            www.salbani.co.uk

St Albans Tourist & Information Centre

The Old Town Hall, Market Place, St Albans, Hertfordshire
     AL3 5DJ
Phone: 01727 864511
Email: tic@stalbans.gov.uk
Web: www.stalbans.gov.uk/tourism/tic.htm

City of St Albans Tour Guides

Web: www.stalbans.gov.uk/tourism/guides/index.htm
For further information and bookings contact the Tourist &
Information Centre

The Lance & Longbow Society

11 Westmeade Close, Rosedale, Cheshunt, Hertfordshire
     EN7 6JP
Phone: 07946 087641
Email: LandLSOC@aol.com
Web: www.lanceandlongbow.com

Livery & Maintenance

Web: www.et-tu.com/livery/cgi-bin/index.cgi/action=John
Nesfield's Retinue

Friends of Bernards Heath

Heath House, Heath Farm Lane, St Albans, Hertfordshire
     AL3 5AE
Email: chairman@bernardsheath.org
Web: www.bernardsheath.org

Richard III Foundation

Web: www.richardiii.net

Wars of the Roses Federation

Web: www.wotrf.org

Appendix B

With comments specific to their roles in the battles.

Key

Y or L	Yorkist or Lancastrian (for each battle). (It has been assumed that all those recorded as dying at the first battle with no other information were Lancastrians.)
1 or 2	First or second battle.
Killed-1	Recorded as killed at the first battle.
Killed-1 (Abbey)	Recorded as killed at the first battle and interred in the Lady Chapel of the Abbey with memorial. (NB: All the graves and monuments in the Abbey were despoiled in the Reformation.)
Wounded-1/2	Recorded as wounded at first/second battle.
<u>Arundel</u>	Underlining indicates the title by which the person is referred to in the main text.

NB:
Please note that many of the references in this Appendix may be uncorroborated.

Name	Code	Notes
Anjou – see Margaret		
William Fitzalan, 9th Earl of Arundel (1417–87)	Y2	
Oliver Atterton and brother (name unknown) (d.1455)	L1	Killed-1 (Abbey)
Sir Ralf Babthorpe (d.1455)	L1	'Second server' to the king in the royal household Killed-1 (Abbey)
Ralf Babthorpe (son of above) (d.1455)	L1	Killed-1, interred in St Peter's Church
Thomas Barker (d.1455)	L1	Killed-1 (Abbey)
Sir James Baskerville	Y1	
John Baytraux/Batryaux/Botreaux (d.1455)	L1	Killed-1 (Abbey)
Beaufort – see Somerset and Dorset		
Sir John Bourchier, 1st Baron Berners, (d.1471)	L?1, Y2	
William Bonville, 1st Baron Bonville (1392–1461)	Y2	Experienced soldier. Charged with guarding Henry VI during second battle and stayed with him afterwards. Executed 18 February on Edward of Lancaster's orders
Bostock – see Whethamstede		
William Botelore/Boteler (d.1455)	L1	Killed-1
Boteler – see Sudeley		
Sir Edward Bourchier (d.1461)	Y1	
Henry Bourchier (Viscount Bourchier and Count of Eu at the time of the battles, created Earl of Essex 1461) (1408–83)	Y?1, Y2	
William Bourchier (d.1472)	Y1	
(no first name) Brecknock	L1	
Brooke – see Cobham		

Name	Code	Notes
Humphrey Stafford, 1st Duke of Buckingham (1402–60)	L1	
William Butler (d.1455)	L1	Killed-1 (Abbey)
Butler – see also Wiltshire		
Sir William Chamberlain (d.1455)	L1	Killed-1 (Abbey)
Richard Chancellor	L1	Killed-1 (Abbey)
Sir Thomas Charleton/Charlton (d.1465)	Y2	Speaker of the House of Commons, captured at second battle
John Child (d.1455)	L1	Killed-1 (Abbey)
John Chilron (d.1455)	L1	Killed-1 (Abbey)
John Clifford, 9th Baron Clifford (1435–61) ('butcher Clifford')	L1, L2	Son of Thomas Clifford. He saw his father killed in first battle. He reunited Henry and Margaret after second battle in some accounts
Thomas Clifford (of Craven), 8th Baron Clifford (Shakespeare's 'Clifford of Cumberland') (1414–55)	L1	Lancastrian commander, killed at one of the Bars in first battle. His body was one of those deliberately left unburied until moved to the Abbey
John Clinton, 5th Lord (de) Clinton of Maxstoke/Maxtock (1410–64)	Y1	
Edward Brooke, 6th Lord Cobham (d.1464)	Y1	
Robert Burton	Y1	
John de Coqina (d.1455)	L1	Killed-1 (Abbey)
William Corbyn/Corvin (d.1455)	L1	Killed-1
William Cotton (d.1455)	L1	Receiver of the Duchy of Lancaster for Norfolk, Suffolk and Cambridgeshire, mentioned in the Paston letters as 'Quotton'. Killed-1
Courtenay – see Devon		
Ralph, 3rd Baron Cromwell (1393–1456)	Y1	

William Curwin (d.1455)	L1	Killed-1 (Abbey)
John Davy (d.1455)	L1	Killed-1 (Abbey)
John Dawes (d.1455)	L1	
John Denston	Y1	
Sir Thomas Courtenay, 13th Earl of Devon (in the Courtney line) (1414–58) (not to be confused with Humphrey Stafford, who became Earl of Devon in 1462)	Y1	
Thomas Courtenay, 14th Earl of Devon (from 1458) (1432–61) (not to be confused with Humphrey Stafford, who became Earl of Devon in 1462)		L2
John Done	L2	Knighted after second battle
Henry Beaufort (1436–64), Earl of Dorset (to 1455) and	L1 as Dorset,	
3rd Duke of Somerset (to 1464)	L2 as Somerset	
John Sutton, 1st Baron Dudley (1400–87)	L1	
Sir Bertine Entwistle (1396–1455)	L1	Died of wounds a few days after first battle and interred in St Peter's Church, St Albans, with a memorial (now lost)
Essex – see Bourchier		
Henry Holland, 2nd Duke of Exeter (1430–75)	(undecided 1) L2	
John Eythe (d.1455)	L1	Killed-1 (same man as John de Herthe?)
Gilbert Faldinger (d.1455)	L1	Killed-1

Name	Code	Notes
Sir William Neville, Lord Fauconberg (and Earl of Kent later in 1461) (1401–63)	L1, Y2	Some authorities place him in St Albans in 1461, making him the only active combatant to change sides between the battles
Sir Ralph Ferrers (d.1455)	L1	Killed-1 (Abbey)
Gilbert Fielding (d.1455)	L1	Killed-1 (Abbey)
Henry Fingley (d.1455)	L1	Killed-1 (Abbey)
Fitzalan – see Arundel		
Henry, 5th Baron Fitzhugh of Ravensworth (1430–72/3)	L2	
Ralph Fitzrandolph	Y1	
Sir Richard Fortescue (d.1455)	L1	Killed-1 (Abbey)
Henry Fylongley/Fenyingley	L1	Wounded-1
John Garthe (d.1455)	L1	Killed-1 (Abbey)
William Gower	Y2	One of Henry VI's standard-bearers at second battle with the Yorkist army. Captured at the battle and executed with Bonville and Kyriel (only mentioned by Sir James Ramsay)
William Gregory (d.1467)	Y2	Chronicler, present at second battle with the Yorkists
Sir Henry Grey, 7th Lord Grey of Codnor (1435–94/6)	L2	
Sir John Grey (of Groby) (entitled to be called Baron Ferrers) (d.1461)	L2	Killed-2, interred in the Abbey. Married to Elizabeth Woodville at the time of the battle
Ralph Greystoke, 5th Baron Greystoke (1414–87)	L2	
Reginald/Reynold Griffin (d.1455)	L1	Killed-1 (Abbey)
Gryphet – see Griffin		
Halyn (no first name) (d.1455)	L1	Henry VI's janitor, killed-1 (Abbey)
Richard Hamerton	Y1	

Symond Hammys	L2	Knighted after second battle
Sir John Hanforth	L1	
Robert Harcourt	L1	
Harpour (no first name) (d.1455)	L1	'Yeoman of the Crown', killed-1
Sir Richard Harrington (d.1455)	L1	Clerk of the king's household, killed-1 alongside Northumberland
Richard Harroden	L1	
(no first name) Hawkin (d.1455)	L1	King's porter, killed-1
Henry VI, Henry Plantagenet, (1421–71) (reigned 1422–61, 1470–1)	L1, L2	
John de Herthe (d.1455)	L1	Killed-1 (Abbey)
Holland – see Exeter		
Thomas Hoo (of Luton Hoo)	Y/L2	'Shield-bearer' to Henry VI at second battle who, according to Whethamstede, negotiated his change of sides on the battlefield
John Howard (6th Duke of Norfolk 1483–5) (1430–85)	Y2	Killed-2
Arnold Hungerford (d.1461)	L2	Killed-2
William Joseph	L1	Blamed, together with Thomas Thorpe, by Yorkists for provoking first battle by bad advice to Henry VI
Sir Thomas Kyriell (1392–1461)	Y2	Charged with guarding Henry VI and stayed with him after second battle. Executed 18 February on Edward of Lancaster's orders
[Sir Thomas Kyriell's] son (d.1461)	Y2	Charged with guarding Henry VI and stayed with him after second battle. Executed next day on Edward of Lancaster's orders. (Mentioned only by Jean de Waurin.)

Edward of Lancaster (Prince of Wales) (1453–71) (also known as Edward of Westminster)	L2	Knighted by Henry VI after second battle, then awarded battle honours to Lancastrian commanders in his turn. Was made to sanction executions on day after the battle
Lovelace of Hurley (Sir Henry Lovelace?)	L2	Reputedly a Kentish squire who was captured at Wakefield and paroled in return for a promise to betray the Yorkists at a future opportunity. Blamed by Warwick for costing him second battle when he caused the vanguard of the main battle to desert in panic. No biographical details known
Henry Loweys (d.1455)	L1	Killed-1 (NB: a Henry Lowys, who had not died in 1455, was a subsequent governor of Henry VI's household)
Sir Thomas Lumley	Y1	
Sir James Lutterell (1426–61)	L2	Died of wounds on 18 February 1461
(no first name) Maleners (d.1455)	L1	Killed-1
Alvercy Malyverer (d.1455)	L1	Killed-1 (Abbey)
Edward Plantagenet, Earl of March, Edward IV 1461–83 (1442–83)	Y1	
Margaret of Anjou (1430–82) (Queen 1445–61, 1470–1)	L2	In London during first battle, acting as regent during the 1461 campaign and directing Lancastrian strategy
Robert Mercroft (d.1455)	L1	'The King's/Queen's Messenger', killed-1
James Metcalfe	Y1	
William Methelan (d.1455)	L1	Killed-1 (Abbey)
John Middleton	Y1	

Name	Battle	Notes
John Neville (Sir John 1453–61, Baron Montagu 1461–4, Earl of Northumberland 1464–70, Marquis of Montagu 1470–71) (1431–71) (also known as 'Montacute')	Y1, Y2	Warwick's brother. Present at first battle but role not recorded. Henry VI's chamberlain by 1461. Commander of a wing at second battle and captured by Lancastrians. Buried at Bisham Abbey (tomb despoiled in the Reformation)
Christopher Moresby	Y1	
Dr (later Cardinal Archbishop) John Morton (d.1500)	L2	Lawyer and priest who became Chancellor to Edward of Lancaster in 1456. With Margaret in 1461 as a political adviser
Mowbray – see Norfolk		
George Neville, Bishop of Exeter and Chancellor of England (1432–76)	Y2	Brother to Warwick and Montagu and with them at second battle
Neville – see also Fauconberg, Montagu, Salisbury and Warwick		
Nicholas (no surname given) (d.1455)	L1	'Of the pantry', killed-1 (Abbey)
John Mowbray, 3rd Duke of Norfolk (1415–61)	undecided 1, Y2	Commanded a Yorkist wing in second battle
Hugh North (d.1455)	Y1	Killed-1 (Abbey)
Henry Percy, 2nd Earl of Northumberland (1394–1455)	L1	Killed-1 (Abbey), then moved to York Minster (both graves despoiled in Reformation)
Henry Percy, 3rd Earl of Northumberland (1421–61)	L2	Co-commander of the Lancastrians at second battle
Sir Robert Ogle (later 1st Baron Ogle) (1406–69)	Y1	Yorkist commander at first battle
Sir William Oldhall (d.1460)	Y1	
Thomas Packington (d.1455)	L1	Swordbearer to the Earl of Northumberland, killed-1, interred in St Peter's Church with memorial (now lost)
(no first name) Padington (d.1455)	L1	Killed-1

John Page (d.1455)	L1	Killed-1 (Abbey)
Malmer Pagentoun (d.1455)	L1	Killed-1
Jasper Tudor, Earl of Pembroke 1453–61, untitled 1461–85, Duke of Bedford 1485–95 (1431–95). (Not to be confused with the Yorkist William Herbert [1432–69], Earl of Pembroke 1461–69)	L1	
Sir Ralph Percy (1425–1464)	L1	
William Percy (Bishop of Carlisle 1452–62)	L1	
Percy – see also Northumberland		
Sir James Pickering (d.1461)	Y1	
de la Pole – see Suffolk		
William Porter (d.1455)	L1	Killed-1 (Abbey)
Sir Robert Poynings (1419–61)	Y2	Commanded Yorkist outpost at Dunstable on 16 February in some accounts. Evicted from there. Killed-2
William Pudsey	Y1	
Robert Purton (d.1455)	L1	Killed-1 (Abbey)
Quotton – see Cotton		
John Radcliffe (d.1455)	L1	Killed-1
John Raulyns-Asple (d.1455)	L1	
William Regmayde (d.1455)	L1	Killed-1
Sir Henry Retford	Y1	
Roke de Westham (d.1455)	L1	Killed-1 (Abbey)
Thomas Ros (or Roos/Rosse/Rose), 9th Baron thereof (1422–64)	L1, L2	Present at first battle, one of the Lancastrian commanders at second. Knighted after the battle

Name	Code	Notes
Edmund Plantagenet, Earl of Rutland (1443–60)	Y1	
Richard Neville, 5th Earl of Salisbury and Earl of Westmorland (1400–60)	Y1	Warwick's father. Leading figure at first battle. Killed at Wakefield 1460, buried at Bisham Abbey (tomb despoiled in the Reformation)
Gilbert Scarebreck/Starbrook/Starbrok/Starlok (d.1455)	L1	William Cotton's squire, killed-1 (Abbey)
Sir Ralph Shirley	L1	
John Talbot, 2nd Earl of Shrewsbury (1413–60)	L1?	
John Talbot, 3rd Earl of Shrewsbury (d.1473)	L2	Son of 2nd Earl, Lancastrian magnate knighted after second battle
Edmund Beaufort, 2nd Duke of Somerset (1406–55) (NB: he is sometimes shown as the 1st Duke of Somerset, but the more common title of 2nd Duke is given here)	L1	Lancastrian commander at first battle, killed-1 (Abbey)
Somerset – see also Dorset		
Lord Humphrey, 'Earl of Stafford' (d.1458)	L1	Buckingham's son, wounded-1
Stafford – see also Buckingham		
Thomas Stanley, 1st Baron Stanley (1406–59)	L1	
Sir Walter Strickland	Y1	
Ralph Boteler, 1st Baron Sudeley (1394–1473)	L1	One of the Lancastrian leaders credited with carrying the royal banner, wounded-1
John de la Pole, 2nd Duke of Suffolk (1442–92)	Y2	
Edmund Sutton	L1	
John Sutton (d.1455)	L1	A clerk, killed-1 (Abbey)
Sutton – see also Dudley		
John Swythman	L1	
Sir William Tailboys of Kyme (1416–64)	L2	Knighted after second battle

Talbot – see Shrewsbury		
John Taylor (d.1455)	L1	Killed-1 (Abbey)
Thomas Thorpe (d.1461)	L1	Speaker of the House of Commons, accused of fleeing first battle. Blamed by the Yorkists, together with William Joseph, for provoking the battle by bad advice to Henry VI
Sir Henry Threlkeld	Y1	
Sir Thomas Tresham (d.1471)	L1, L2	Speaker of the House of Commons, Usher of the king's household in 1455 and Comptroller in 1461, knighted after second battle
Andrew Trollope (d.1461)	L2	Professional soldier from the Calais garrison. Wounded by a caltrop. Knighted on battlefield by Edward of Lancaster
Tudor – see Pembroke		
Henry Unton	Y1	
Sir Robert Vere (d.1455)	L1	Killed-1 (Abbey)
James Wandesford	Y1	
Richard West, 7th Baron de la Warre/Warr (d.1475/6)	L2	
Richard Neville, Earl of Warwick ('Warwick the Kingmaker') (1428–71)	Y1, Y2	Leading Yorkist magnate at first battle and Yorkist commander at second. Buried at Bisham Abbey (tomb despoiled in the Reformation)
Lionel Welles, 6th Baron Welles (1406–61)	L2	
Richard Welles, 7th Baron Willoughby, 7th Baron Welles, (1428–70) (NB: in some accounts Welles and Willoughby are accounted two separate people, but the titles were held by the one man 1461–70)	L2	Son of Lionel Welles
Sir John Wenlock (1st Baron Wenlock) (d.1471)	L1	Speaker of the House of Commons, wounded-1

Name	Code	Notes
Sir Philip Wentworth (d.1464)	L1	One of the Lancastrian leaders credited with carrying the royal banner, but fled the field
Richard West	L1	
West – see also de la Warr/Warre		
Westmorland – see Salisbury		
Abbot John Whethamstede (several variations) (1392–1465) (also known as John Bostock)	L1, Y2	Eyewitness to both battles
Robert Whytynham/ Whitingham (d.1471)	L2	Knighted after second battle
William (no surname given) (d.1455)	Y1	Baker to the Duke of York, killed-1 (Abbey)
William Willeflete	Y1	Duke of York's confessor and important messenger at first battle
John Willoughby (d.1455)	L1	Killed-1 (Abbey)
Raufe Willerby/Ralph Willoughby (d.1455)	L1	
James Butler, 1st Earl of Wiltshire and 5th Earl of Ormond (1420–61)	L1	Fled battlefield disguised as a monk
Lias de Wood (or Elys Woode) (d.1455)	L1	Killed-1 (Abbey)
Robert Woodward (d.1455)	L1	Killed-1 (Abbey)
Richard Plantagenet, 3rd Duke of York (1411–60)	Y1	Royal Duke and Yorkist commander, at first battle
John Zouche (d.1455)	L1	Killed-1 (Abbey)
William Zouche (d.1455)	L1	

FURTHER READING

THERE IS A GREAT DEAL of primary material on the battles – though not all of it very coherent and focused – and a vast body of secondary material on the Wars of the Roses and on the two battles. This list cites the references specifically made to these sources in the text (and primary sources relied on even if not quoted) and goes on to suggest those more important works used by the authors and which a more general reader might also wish to follow up.

Primary Sources: General

Benet's Chronicle, quoted in Hallam (ed.), *Chronicles of the Wars of the Roses*

The Croyland Chronicle Continuations 1459–1486, eds N. Ponay and J. Cox, Richard III and Yorkist History Trust, Alan Sutton, 1986

Dockray, K., *Henry VI, Margaret of Anjou and the Wars of the Roses: a Source Book*, Sutton Publishing Ltd, 2000

Douglas, D. C. (ed.), *English Historical Documents*, vol. IV: *1327–1485*, Eyre and Spottiswood, 1969

An English Chronicle of the Reigns of Richard II, Henry IV, Henry V, and Henry VI, ed. J. S. Davies, Camden Society, 1856

Fabyan, R., *The New Chronicles of England and France*, ed. H. Ellis, 1811 (first published 1516)

The Great Chronicle of London, eds A. H. Thomas and I. E. Thornley, 1938 (compiled 1512)

Hall, E., *Hall's Chronicle: containing the History of England …*, ed. H. Ellis, 1890 (first published 1550)

Hallam, E. (ed.), *Chronicles of the Wars of the Roses*, Weidenfeld and Nicolson, 1988

Holinshed, Raphael, *Chronicles of England*, eds A. and J. Nicoll, Everyman, 1965 (first published 1577)

Mancini, D., *The Usurpation of Richard III*, ed. C. A. J. Armstrong, Clarendon Press (2nd edn), 1969 (first published 1483)

Waurin (or Wavrin), J. de, *Anchiennes Chroniques d'Engleterre*, 3 vols, ed. E. Dupont, Société de l'Histoire de France, 1858–63 (compiled 1470)

Whethampstede, Abbot J., *Registrum Abbatiae*, ed. H. T. Riley, English Historical Rolls Series, 1872 (compiled at the time of the events)

Worcestre, W., *Annales Rerum Anglicarum*, in Douglas, *English Historical Documents*, vol. IV

Primary Sources: First Battle

The Dijon Relation, Archives de la Côte d'Or, B. 11942, no. 258, Dijon, in Armstrong, *Politics and the Battle of St. Albans, 1455* and in Lander, *The Wars of the Roses*

Phillips, *Extract from the Phillips Relation*, in *The Paston Letters 1422–1509*, ed. J. Gairdner, Constable and Co., 1895

Rotuli Parliamentorum, vol. V, p. 282, Record Commission, in Douglas, *English Historical Documents*

Stow, J., *The Stow Relation: The Stonor Variant*, in *The Paston Letters 1422–1509*, ed. J. Gairdner, Constable and Co., 1895

Stow, J., *The Stow Relation: The Vale Variant*, in Kekewich et al., *The Politics of Fifteenth-Century England: John Vale's Book*

Worcestre, W., *Itineraries*, ed. J. H. Harvey, Oxford University Press, 1989 (compiled 1477–80, first published 1544)

Primary Sources: Second Battle

Calendar of State Papers and Manuscripts existing in the Archives and Collections of Milan, vol. I, ed. A. B. Hinds, 1912

Calendar of State Papers and Manuscripts relating to English Affairs existing in the Archives and Collections of Venice, vol. I: *1202–1509*, ed. R. Brown, Longmans, 1864

Gregory, W., *Chronicle*, ed. J. Gairdner, Camden Society, 1876 (compiled 1469)

Secondary Sources

Armstrong, C. A. J., *Politics and the Battle of St. Albans, 1455*, Bulletin of the Institute of Historical Research, vol. 33, 1960

Ashdown, C. H., *The Battles and Battlefields of St. Albans, 1455–1461*, Gibbs and Bamforth, 1913

Auckland, R. G., *The Second Battle of St Albans 1461*, privately printed, 1992 (partly reproduced at www.sandridgevillage.com/history/history10.cfm)

Bennett, M., 'The Development of Battle Tactics in the Hundred Years War', in A. Curry and M. Hughes (eds), *Arms, Armies and Fortifications in the Hundred Years War*, Woodbridge, 1994

Boardman, A., *The First Battle of St Albans 1455*, Tempus Publishing, 2006

Brook, R., *Cassel's Battlefields of Britain and Ireland*, Weidenfeld and Nicolson, 2005

Burne, A. H., *The Battlefields of England*, Methuen, 1950

Cole, H., *The War of the Roses*, Hart-Davis, 1975

Dixon, J., 'The Second Battle of St Albans', unpublished paper

Evans, H. T., *Wales and the Wars of the Roses*, Sutton Publishing, 1998

Featherstone, D. F., *The Bowmen of England*, Pen and Sword Books, 2003

Goodman, A., *The Wars of the Roses: Military Activity and English Society, 1452–97*, Routledge and Kegan Paul, 1982

Green, Col. H., 'Battlefields Then and Now: the First Battle of St. Albans, 1455', *Military Modelling*, June 1979

Hackett, M., *Lost Battlefields of Britain*, Sutton Publishing, 2005

Haigh, P. A., *The Military Campaigns of the Wars of the Roses*, Sutton Publishing, 1995

Hampton, W. E., *Memorials of the Wars of the Roses*, Alan Sutton, 1979

Harrison, I., *British Battles*, Getmapping, 2002

Hicks, M. A., 'Propaganda and the First Battle of St Albans', *Nottingham Medieval Studies Journal*, 44, 2000

Hicks, M. A., *Warwick the Kingmaker*, Blackwell, 1998

Kekewich, M. L. et al., *The Politics of Fifteenth-Century England: John Vale's Book*, Alan Sutton, 1995

Kendall, P., *Warwick the Kingmaker*, Allen and Unwin, 1957

Lander, J. R., *The Wars of the Roses*, Sutton Publishing, 1990

Maurer, H. E., *Margaret of Anjou*, Boydell Press, 2003

Maxfield, Father Stephen, 'What Happened to the Dead Bodies after a Medieval Battle?', *Battlefield*, vol. 11, issue 1, Battlefields Trust, 2005

McGlynn, S., 'The Myths of Medieval Warfare', *History Today*, vol. 44, no. 1, 1994

Neillands, R., *The Wars of the Roses*, Cassell, 1992

Norwich, J. J., *Shakespeare's Kings*, Penguin, 2000

Pollard, A., 'The Battle of St Albans, 1455', *History Today*, vol. 55, no. 5, 2005

Ramsay, Sir James H., *York and Lancaster*, vol. 2, Clarendon, 1895

Rayner, M., *English Battlefields*, Tempus, 2004

Richardson, G., *A Pride of Bastards*, Basildon Books, 2002

Richmond, C., 'The Nobility and the Wars of the Roses 1459–61', *Nottingham Medieval Studies*, 21, 1977

Ross, C. R., *Edward IV*, Methuen, 1983

Schama, S., *A History of Britain*, vol. 1, BBC, 2000

Seymour, W., *Battles in Britain and their Political Background*, vol. 1: *1066–1547*, Sidgwick and Jackson, 1979

Shakespeare, W., *Henry VI Part 2* (Act 1, Scene IV and Act 5, Scene II) (first published 1594)

Shaw, W. A., *The Knights of England*, 2 vols, Heraldry Today, 1906 (reprinted 1971)

Smith, R. D. and de Vries, K., *The Artillery of the Dukes of Burgundy, 1363–1477*, Boydell Press, 2005

Smurthwaite, D., *The Ordnance Survey Complete Guide to the Battlefields of Britain*, Webb and Bower, 1984

Strickland, M. and Hardy, R., *The Great Warbow, from Hastings to the Mary Rose*, Sutton Publishing, 2005

Thornley, I. D., *England under the Yorkists 1460–1485*, University of London Intermediate Source Books no. 2, 1921

Wagner, J. A., *Encyclopedia of the Wars of the Roses*, ABC-CLIO, 2001

Weever, J., *Ancient Funeral Monuments*, 1631 (reprinted by Theatrum Orbis Terrarum, 1979)

Weir, A., *Lancaster and York: the Wars of the Roses*, Jonathan Cape, 1995

Wetherell, J. E., *Fields of Fame in England and Scotland*, Macmillan, 1923

Local History Bibliography
(including online resources)

Alvey, N., 'Growth in the Population of St Albans from the Seventeenth to the Nineteenth Centuries', *The Local Historian*, vol. 30, no. 3, 2000, www.balh.co.uk/tlh

Carbery, M., *Happy World*, Longmans, 1941

Carrington, B. and Thresher, M., *The Ghost Book: St Albans' Favourite Haunts* (no publisher or date, but probably St Albans 1993)

Chauncy, Sir Henry, *The Historical Antiquities of Hertfordshire*, vol. 2, Kohler and Coombs, 1975 (first published 1700)

Hodson, D. (ed.), *Four County Maps of Hertfordshire*, Hertfordshire Publications, 1985

McSweeney, G., 'Hall Place and the First Battle of St. Albans, 22 May 1455', *Herts Past and Present*, 3rd series, issue no. 6, 2005

Niblett, R. and Thompson, I., *Alban's Buried Towns*, Oxbow Books/English Heritage, 2005

Reynolds, C. F., *A Short History of Bernards Heath*, Codil Language Systems, 2000

Shrimpton, J., *Antiquities of Verulam and St Albans* (c.1631), ed. C. I. A. Ritchie (reprinted by the St Albans and Hertfordshire Architectural and Archaeological Society, 1966)

Swinson, C., *The St Albans Pageant: the Masque of the Queens. Souvenir Programme*, Gainsborough Press, 1953 (containing the full text of a dramatization of the second battle)

Tompkins, H., *Highways and Byways in Hertfordshire*, Macmillan, 1902 (representative of the many antiquarian-cum-travelogue books mentioning the battles in the nineteenth and twentieth centuries)

Toms, E., *The Story of St Albans*, White Crest, 1962
Wright, P., 'Time and Tithes', *History Today*, vol. 54, no. 8, 2004
www.hertsheritage.org.uk/transport/rom.htm (for Roman roads)

Online Resources
(accessed winter 2005 – spring 2006)

Bothwell, Dr J., *Patrons and Patronised Relationships: Affinity and 'Bastard Feudalism'*, University of Leicester, www.le.ac.uk/hi/jsb16/patronage.htm
Buckingham's Retinue, www.bucks-retinue.org.uk
Ellis, T., *Ghosts of the South East, Part One*, Mercian Order of St George, http://members.aol.com/MercStG2/GOSEENGPage1.html
Encyclopedia of Historical Weapons, www.armouronline.com/encyclopedia_of_historical_weapons
Miller, M. D., *Wars of the Roses*, www.warsoftheroses.co.uk
Oxford University Press, *Dictionary of National Biography*, www.oup.com/oxforddnb/info/online
Price, B. (trans.), *How a Man Shall be Armyd*, Archeologia 57, part I, www.chronique.com/Library/Armour/armyd1.htm
Richard III Foundation, www.richard111.com

Index